From the pages of *The Art of War*

"The art of war is of vital importance to the State. It is a matter
of life and death, a road either to safety or to ruin. Hence it is a
subject of inquiry which can on no account be neglected."
(chapter I, paragraphs 1–2)

"All warfare is based on deception."
(chapter I, paragraph 18)

"There is no instance of a country having
benefited from prolonged warfare."
(chapter II, paragraph 6)

"Hence to fight and conquer in all your battles is not supreme
excellence; supreme excellence consists in
breaking the enemy's resistance
without fighting."
(chapter III, paragraph 2)

"If you know the enemy and know yourself, you need not
fear the result of a hundred battles. If you know yourself but not
the enemy, for every victory gained you will also suffer a defeat.
If you know neither the enemy nor yourself, you
will succumb in every battle."
(chapter III, paragraph 18)

"We cannot enter into alliances until we are acquainted with
the designs of our neighbours."
(chapter VII, paragraph 12)

"Rapidity is the essence of war."
(chapter XI, paragraph 19)

"If the enemy leaves a door open, you must rush in."
(chapter XI, paragraph 65)

"Be subtle! Be subtle! and use your spies for
every kind of business."
(chapter XIII, paragraph 18)

法兵子孫

THE
ART OF WAR

~∽~

SUN TZU

Edited with an Introduction by
DALLAS GALVIN

Translated from the Chinese by
LIONEL GILES,
with his Notes and Commentaries
from the Chinese Masters

George Stade
Consulting Editorial Director

JB
BARNES & NOBLE CLASSICS
NEW YORK

$\mathcal{B}$

BARNES & NOBLE CLASSICS

NEW YORK

Published by Barnes & Noble Books
122 Fifth Avenue
New York, NY 10011

www.barnesandnoble.com/classics

Lionel Giles's translation of Sun Tzu's *The Art of War* was first published in 1910.

Originally published in 2003 by Barnes & Noble Classics with new Introduction, Notes, Biography, Chronology, Inspired By, Index, and For Further Reading. This hardcover edition published in 2004.

The Art of War
ISBN-13: 978-1-59308-172-0
ISBN-10: 1-59308-172-3
LC Control Number 2004100760

Produced and published in conjunction with:
Fine Creative Media, Inc.
322 Eighth Avenue
New York, NY 10001

Michael J. Fine, President and Publisher

Printed in the United States of America
MV
9   10   8

Sun Tzu

STRATEGY, ESPIONAGE, DECEPTION, military tactics—these are the themes elucidated in the ancient Chinese text *The Art of War*, the indispensable handbook to a subject that has occupied kings and generals for millennia. Little is known about the historical figure of the book's author, Sun Tzu. The earliest accounts of his life were written hundreds of years after he died, and the surviving information is clouded by legend.

Thought to have lived in the fifth century B.C., at roughly the same time as Confucius, Sun Tzu was born as Sun Wu—Sun was his family name, Wu his given name, and Tzu an honorific title. His family was part of a clan of experts on arms and fighting; in that era, clans and families "owned" information, just as in the medieval European guilds fathers passed on specialized knowledge and training to their sons. Sun Tzu's teachings are most likely a combination of his clan's ideas and his own, as well as concepts associated with early Taoism.

Throughout ancient times, the political and social climate of China was characterized by violent upheaval, the rise and fall of great dynasties, and almost continuous military conflict. Sun Tzu followed the profession of his clan and, on the basis of his growing reputation, entered the service of Ho Lu, king of the state of Wu, as a traveling adviser for hire. His military stratagems intrigued the king, and Sun Tzu eventually became general of the king's army. Employing psychology, deceit, strategic power, and diplomacy as the fundamental arts of combat, Sun Tzu defeated numerous opponents and created a systematic treatise on war.

Military history offers dramatic testimony of Sun Tzu's wisdom—the adoption of his methods by the leaders of history's great armies, and the failure of those who disregarded them.

TABLE OF CONTENTS

THE WORLD OF SUN TZU AND
THE ART OF WAR

c.1700–c.1027 B.C. The Shang Dynasty is the first documented Chinese civilization. Cities are built, and writing and techniques of bronze metallurgy are developed.

c.1027 The Chou Dynasty begins. The golden age of Chinese philosophy, including the works of Confucius and Lao Tze, it will last until 221 B.C. The first part of the Chou Dynasty, known as the Western Chou Dynasty, will last until 772 B.C., when the Chinese rulers are forced east by barbarians from the north; the king is killed, but his son establishes a new capital at Loyang.

772 The Eastern Chou Dynasty begins; its first part, the Spring and Autumn period, is a time of continuous wars for survival among many small city-states. The Chou emperor steadily loses power as the feudal lords realize he can be beaten, as proved by the defeat in the west. By the end of the Spring and Autumn period (around 481 B.C.) only about a dozen consolidated central states will remain.

685–643 An early state hegemony is established under Duke Huan of Qi. He introduces new state institutions such as taxation, a state-funded army, and state ownership of natural resources; he also establishes an alliance of central states to oppose the power of the large southern kingdom of Chu.

632 A new hegemony of Jin is established under Duke Wen.

c.551 Confucius is born in the northern state of Lu. Over the course of his life, he rises from a warehouse manager to become one of history's best-known teachers.

546 The state of Sun, which is bordered by the warring states of Chu and Jin, invites a delegation of eleven states to sign a nonaggression pact. The peace lasts forty years and gives the larger states a reprieve from several hundred years of constant war.

544 Sun Wu is born in the state of Chi. Later he will be given the honorific title Sun Tzu, meaning Master Sun.

514 The rule of King Ho Lu of the state of Wu begins.

510 Sun Tzu enters the service of Ho Lu.

506 The forty-year peace brokered by the state of Sun in 546 B.C. is broken by the state of Wu, which was not part of the peace agreement.

500 To defend against marauding barbarians from the north, the northern Chinese states begin building walls that are later connected to form the Great Wall of China.

496 King Ho Lu dies of wounds sustained in battle. Although Sun Tzu's death is never confirmed, it is assumed he did not outlive the king.

482 Wu gains power and becomes the dominant state in ancient China.

479 Confucius dies, leaving many followers who spread his teachings about the proper management of society, based on sympathy or "human-heartedness."

472 The state of Wu is defeated by the upstart state of Yue.

c.403 The Eastern Chou Dynasty's Warring States period begins; it is characterized by a power struggle between the large states of China, each trying to gain control over the entire area. The Warring States period will last until the end of the Chou Dynasty, about 221 B.C.

c.380 Sun Pin, a descendant of Sun Tzu, is born. Sun Pin is the supposed author of *The Lost Art of War*, which is considered a companion piece to *The Art of War*. Sun Pin will achieve great fame as a general, and his writings will build on ideas and tactics found in Sun Tzu's seminal work.

221 B.C. China is unified under the harsh rule of Ch'in Shih Huang-ti. The Chou Dynasty ends and the Ch'in Dynasty begins. Bureaucratic government is established, and a written language is standardized. Roads and canals are built, as is much of the Great Wall.

91 The *Shih Chi* (Historical Records), the first known history of China, is completed. It includes one of two ancient biographies of Sun Tzu.

1st century A.D. The *Wu Yueh Ch'un-ch'iu* appears. It contains a biography of Sun Tzu that details his fabled arrival into the service of King Ho Lu. The *Wu Yueh Ch'un-ch'iu* is entertaining, but it is most likely a romanticized embellishment of the tales found in the *Shih Chi*.

1772 *The Art of War* is translated into French by Father J. J. Amiot, a Jesuit who learned of Sun Tzu and *The Art of War* while he was a missionary in China. The translation is probably read by Napoleon.

1905 In Tokyo, the first English translation of *The Art of War*, by Captain E. F. Calthrop, appears under the title *Sonshi*, the Japanese form of Sun Tzu.

1910 Lionel Giles publishes his English translation of *The Art of War*.

1972 An archaeological dig unearths a lost text of *The Art of War* in the Shantung province of modern China. The text contains long sections of thirteen chapters that are already known as well as passages from five lost chapters. The texts appear to have been buried around 140 B.C.

INTRODUCTION

It is mere illusion and pretty sentiment to expect much from mankind if it forgets how to make war. As yet no means are known which call so much into action as a great war, that rough energy born of the camp, that deep impersonality born of hatred, that conscience born of murder and cold-bloodedness, that fervor born of effort in the annihilation of the enemy, that proud indifference to loss, to one's own existence, to that of one's fellows, to that earthquake-like soul-shaking which a people needs when it is losing its vitality.

Friedrich Wilhelm Nietzsche, *Human, All Too Human* (1878)

———————

War . . . is in its essence, and it is a main condition of its success, to kindle into fierce exercise among great masses of men the destructive and combative passions—passions as fierce and malevolent as that with which the hound hunts the fox to its death. . . . Destruction is one of its chief ends. Deception is one of its chief means, and one of the great arts of skillful generalship is to deceive in order to destroy. . . . It would be difficult to conceive a disposition more remote from the morals of ordinary life, not to speak of Christian ideals. . . . Hardly any one will be so confident of the virtue of his rulers as to believe that every war . . . is just and necessary.

W. E. H. Lecky, *The Map of Life* (1899)

✦ ✦ ✦

WAR IS A HOWLING, BAYING JACKAL. Or is it the animating storm? Suicidal madness or the purifying fire? An imperialist travesty? Or the glorious explosion of a virile nation made manifest upon the planet? In all recorded history, this debate is recent, as is the idea of peace to describe an active state happier than a mere interregnum between fisticuffs. Astounding as it may seem, war has consistently won the debate. In fact, it never had serious competition—not until August 24, 1898, anyway, when Czar Nicholas II of Russia called for an international conference specifically to discuss "the most effectual means" to "a real and durable peace." That was the first time nations would gather without a war at their backs to discuss how war might be prevented systematically. Nicholas was successful. His first Peace Conference was held in 1899. It was followed by a second, in 1907. These meetings gave rise to a process in which the world gained a common code of international laws.

It was a moment when peace and the trials of war were under the microscope of the civilized world. Off in a very quiet corner of this stage, there also appeared two scholars: one, a ghost, Sun Wu—this is Sun Tzu's actual name; Sun is the family name, and Tzu an honorific—a member of a Chinese clan of experts on arms and fighting, who had lived some 2,400 years earlier; the other, a librarian and student of the Chinese classics, Lionel Giles, who published his translation of *The Art of War* in 1910. He, too, was a son of eminence—his father was the great sinologist Herbert Giles—and he transported Sun Tzu's urgent injunctions on the nature of war across vast reaches of time and culture; the task was extraordinary, the impetus behind it almost saintly. The influence of the work of these two men colors our lives even as this text is written. But it did not come without effort, and even today, with a century of English-language scholarship on Asian literature, religion, and societies behind us, there is still much to puzzle the general reader.

World War I and its carnage would soon burst upon the world, leaving an estimated 25 million dead, twice the tally for *all* the wars of nineteenth-century Europe. Nicholas and his entire class would disappear amid the terrors of revolution in Russia, China, and Mexico, to name but the grandest uprisings. World War II would follow with no fewer than 60 million dead, and on its heels a whirl of wars for independence, civil wars, and the surrogate wars of Vietnam, Korea, Africa, the Balkans, and the Middle East—all in all, a century-long testament to the failure of humanity's best intentions. It would be an odd soul who did not find himself feeling as Abraham Lincoln did in his Second Inaugural Address, on March 4, 1865, as the American Civil War was ending: "Fondly do we hope—fervently do we pray—that this mighty scourge of war may speedily pass away."

Yet it takes little experience to understand the futility of belligerence alone, as Sun Tzu wrote: "[H]e who is destined to defeat first fights and afterwards looks for victory" (chap. IV, paragraph 15). On the world front or the level of the individual, the issue is not force, not arms—it is strategy. In his study of Mao Tse-tung, modern warfare's most ardent student of Sun Tzu, Robert Payne notes: "Sun Wu's ideas on war are exceedingly adaptable, . . . nearly all of them demonstrating how the commander of a small force can overcome a powerful enemy, given suitable conditions of his own making. These apothegms have a peculiarly Chinese flavor, hardheaded, deeply philosophical, often showing a disturbing knowledge of the human soul under stress" (Robert Payne, *Mao Tse-tung*; see "For Further Reading"). But how did Sun Tzu know what he knew? Where did he get his information? Can we trust it?

Sometime (most historians suggest about 500 B.C.) during the Spring and Autumn period of the Eastern Chou Dynasty (see section "The World of Sun Tzu and *The Art of War*"), a strikingly serious fellow, dressed in simple monkish gray, the living man named Sun Tzu, contemplated the madness of his times as deeply and clearly as he could. According to modern Chinese scholars, Sun Tzu belonged to an extended family whose members for generations had made their living as military advisers. The revelations Sun Tzu provides us would have been a combination of the journeyman ideas taught (and preserved) by his clan, as well as his own. He would also have been imbued with the ideas we associate with Taoism, which were very much a part of the times.

Foremost among them for a supremely disciplined military adviser like Sun Tzu would have been two commands, both of which required methodical and deliberate decisions. First is the mandate for the strong and the knowledgeable to help the weak. Evening out the playing field carried the charge of religious duty for these advisers. Along with that comes the question of virtue, "the mandate of Heaven." That meant Sun Tzu would have assessed the intrinsic virtue of the weaker and the stronger powers, adhering to the rule of *t'ien ming*, "the mandate of Heaven," as described in the Classical Chinese text *The Book of Documents*. As Burton Watson explains, would-be conquerors, "by their just and virtuous actions, receive from Heaven—a vague, half-personalized spiritual power which rules the universe—a command to set up a new rule. So long as the successive leaders of the new dynasty continue to follow the virtuous course which first entitled their predecessors to the mandate, Heaven will continue to sanction their power." But if they do not maintain virtue, all bets are off: If they sink into "negligence and evil," Heaven will bestow its sanction upon another group of leaders. "In other words, it is virtue alone that entitles a ruler to rule, and when he sets aside virtue, he sets aside the right to call himself a sovereign. The throne is conferred . . . only for as long as the dynasty proves worthy of it" (Watson, *Early Chinese Literature*). Sun Tzu would have considered these issues quite seriously. Even given the frailty of all human flesh, sayings equivalent to our common phrases "It's not my problem" and "It's just business" or even the excuse of the "tyranny of the bottom line" would have been unthinkable.

The resulting document—for Sun Tzu was a man of the aristocracy and could write—is a treatise that has come down through history to be called *Sun-tzu ping-fa*, *Sun Tzu on the Art of War*, just *Sun Tzu* (the customary nomenclature the Chinese use instead of a book title), or, as in many modern editions, *The Art of War*. For Sun Tzu, war, like most of mankind's social, biological, and financial activities, followed certain patterns that can be distilled into laws. He codified his observations into the first military treatise in recorded history. Significantly, he was not only the first to teach that the side that controls those laws of engagement wins, but the long-term influence of his and certain other texts meant that Imperial China, once it had taken shape, rarely needed to wage war outside its boundaries. At the time Lionel Giles made his translation, in fact, China was considered something of a teddy bear among the bellicose hotheads of empire. So Giles in this translation is braiding the two warring streams of thought about war—that it is senseless butchery and that it serves as a sacred restorative to the body politic—into a work that cautions against war, then argues for how it may best be carried out. This is an extraordinary document at an extraordinary turning point in world history.

Equally important, though perhaps startling to Western ears, is the statement that Sun Tzu was a humanist. He advocated waging fast, offensive wars, once one had made deliberate calculations and decided that war was the only reasonable alternative. Why? Fewer deaths, less destruction of the countryside, and thus less hardship on the farmers who lived there and worked the land. This was humanism with an edge, however, since farmers and peasants also serve as conduits for information and sources for food and shelter for armies in the field. Moreover—and this has inspired American as well as Asian generals—Sun Tzu taught that the less destruction of the land, people, and infrastructure, the more the victor would gain, and the easier it would be to convert the vanquished into citizens, not rebels.

A digression on the major centers of civilization might be helpful here: At the time Sun Tzu trod the earth, China would have been evolving for nearly two millennia. Europe and Russia were barbarian lands and Mesopotamia was in decline, but Athens was at its ascendance—this is about the time of the Peloponnesian Wars. India was well developed, with a highly organized social structure. Indeed, though it would fix on class issues more than actual combat, by about 300 B.C. what might be called the Indian *Art of War*, the *Artha Sastra*, would be composed by Kautilya.

Thanks to the intrepid work of anthropologists and archaeologists, not to mention the Chinese passion for compiling historical records, we know something of the times and the culture of 500 B.C. China already possessed a written language and most of the characteristics that made it one of the most advanced empires on the planet. Well before 1600 B.C., the Chinese had invented and were using metal casting. By Sun Tzu's time, though they did not work gold, they produced exquisite jade objects, jewelry, unsurpassed ceramics, and huge bronze statues. They had horse-drawn chariots and formidable weapons of war.

The Chinese were not explorers or wanderers. Others, often barbarians, came to them, especially along the fabled Silk Road, but the Chinese did not travel much until historical times. Early on, they founded scores of complex cities, arranged with three well-defined areas situated within or behind retaining walls; these protective walls often figure in Sun Tzu's calculations. For example, the wall of Chou was made of pounded earth 30 feet high and 40 feet thick. Any general would have to think hard about surmounting that! The typical urban layout, according to historian J. M. Roberts (*A Short History of the World*), was "a small enclosure where the aristocracy lived, a larger one, inhabited by specialized craftsmen and merchants, and the fields outside which fed the city." Commerce bustled and mercantile streets included jewelry, food and clothing shops, and "taverns, gambling houses, and brothels."

Every commentator, however, will point out that for all the wonders of its cities, the heart of Chinese society is in the countryside. The power of the landowners over the peasants as well as the land during the time when Sun Tzu wrote is difficult to imagine for those who have experienced the rootlessness of contemporary society. The aristocracy not only controlled the land much as feudal lords would some 1,000 years later in Europe, but they owned the carts, the livestock, the implements, and even the people. As Roberts points out, adding an important dimension to Sun Tzu's advice to generals in encouraging troops: "Labourers could be sold, exchanged, or left by will"; in other words, many members of the infantry would have been serfs. Also, in those times the nobleman always had a monopoly on armaments, and "only noblemen could afford the weapons, armour, and horses [of war]."

Highly developed as Chinese culture was, the era of the Spring and Autumn period, during which Sun Tzu composed his treatise, was outstandingly brutal. More than one hundred feudal states and principalities were reduced to about forty, in a process that continued until about 403 B.C., when the state of Ch'in officially split into three parts and there were only seven important states left. The year began the Warring States period, which ended in the unification of the empire under Ch'in Shih-huang-ti, the first emperor of the Ch'in Dynasty, who took power in 221 B.C.

Classical Chinese at the time Sun Tzu wrote was a matter of "pronouncements," as was also true in early Western and Near Eastern civilizations; consider, for example, the pithy maxims of Marcus Aurelius and Hesiod. And particularly in the case of documents such as Sun Tzu's military treatise, clans and families in a sense "owned" information—just as in medieval European guilds fathers passed on their goldsmithing or other specialized training and lore to their sons; the transmission of this information was accomplished in both physical and verbal lessons. A written version would have served solely as a mnemonic, and the language was therefore often startling and symbolic, like poetry.

Further, both as an aid to memory and also because of the

intrinsic characteristics of the language, which consists of single syllables ending in mutable vowel sounds, there is a tendency in Chinese writing "to use balanced, parallel phrases, and to treat ideas in the form of numerical categories—the five felicities, the three virtues, etc." (*Early Chinese Literature*). This gives the language an unparalleled drive and power but, as with poetry, makes it almost impossible to translate while retaining its original efficiency and style. And in a strong divergence from the Western Romantic ideal, the Chinese made no distinction between *belles lettres* and didactic literature, between philosophy, say, and storytelling or military treatises. The Emperor Wan of Wei even referred to literature as "a vital force in the ordering of the state."

The distinguishing mark of writing was its refinement or its vulgarity of expression. "Good" meant works of whatever stripe that were "morally sound in content, clear in thought, and expressed in suitably gracious and dignified language" (*Early Chinese Literature*). Meanwhile readers avidly sought works—this is also characteristic of high culture in Greece and India—that explored what the twentieth-century poet Stephen Spender (in *The Making of a Poem*) would call "that human experience so neglected in modern art—the art of ruling, the art of being a prince and being responsible for the use of power."

The moral and social content of the ancient Chinese world was thoroughly scrutinized and reflected upon by Sun Tzu. As a result, his was an approach to human frailty so elastic and capacious—and so true not just to the Chinese, but to the human way—that it sits easily with Western and Eastern military establishments, and still can form the basis for hilarious, long-running Korean sitcoms, kung-fu action flicks, sight gags in Hollywood comedies, countless boost-your-aggression-quotient tomes by business-school professors, and cusp-of-religious-enquiry books. It's been an endless marvel since its first "publication" some 2,500 years ago.

For writers in the West from Hugo Grotius (*De jure belli et pacis*, 1625) to President Theodore Roosevelt (*The Winning of the West*, 1889), wars, like the great forest fires of summer, cleanse society of its Darwinian detritus and give backbone to those who survive. John Milton's Satan distilled it as: "th' unconquerable will, / And study of revenge, immortal hate, / And courage never to submit or yield / And what is else not to be overcome?" (*Paradise Lost*, book 1). If we learn about war from the movies, in which heroes rise from innumerable wounds in seconds flat to fight with nary a shiver of fear, it does seem a clean, albeit loud, exercise, and reading the clipped, clear pronouncements of Sun Tzu would make it seem all the easier. But historically war is synonymous with mud and thorns, with dysentery, typhoid, and famine. The best military minds may disagree on many points, but on one they will always concur: The only way to prevent war is to know how to wage and win it better than your enemy. So, first, let us examine what we think war is, how it is defined, and then proceed to how it is waged.

West or East, Asia or Europe, war conjures deception as much as destruction. The old High German word for war—the root of the English word—was *werre*, "to confound." And wars, as opposed to beer-hall brawls, are not a "blind struggle between mobs of people" but rather an engagement or a series of them between well-organized masses, moving as a team, acting under a single, overarching will, and directed against a definite objective: another country or alliance of countries. This definition (adapted from the *Encyclopedia Britannica*, eleventh edition) is key.

The nineteenth-century Prussian scholar Carl von Clausewitz amplifies that description to give us a precise understanding of tactics versus strategy in his monumental work *Vom Kriege* (On War):

> The conduct of war . . . consists in the planning and conduct of fighting. . . . [Fighting] consists of a greater or lesser number of single acts, each complete in itself, . . . called "engagements." . . . This gives rise to the completely different activity of planning and executing these engagements themselves, and of coordinating each of them with the others in order to further the object of the war. One has been called tactics, and the other, strategy.

Wars are political. They derive from the will of one *polis*, or people, against another, usually in a contest to determine which will exercise sovereignty over land, as in territorial wars, or beliefs, as in religious or ideological wars. Either way, war requires a definite objective and a definite enemy. Terrorism is not war; it is an important tactic of war. The distinction is neither arbitrary nor small. To give some recent examples: Terrorism was used with extraordinary efficiency by the Nazis in World War II (a large invading nation against a weaker one), by the would-be Israelis in their quest for statehood from England (a small force against a larger one), and by France as it battled Algerian independence fighters (a large force against a weaker one). The scholar Francis Dummer Fisher, cited by historian Barbara Fields (*Humane Letters: Writing in English About Human Affairs*, 2003), writes, "War is not defined by damage, however great, but by an intent to conquer." Professor Fields, an expert on the American Civil War at Columbia University, continues:

> Just as mass murder is not necessarily terrorism, so mass murder and terrorism are not necessarily war. Indeed, their perpetrators often choose mass murder and terrorism precisely for lack of the political standing, power, resources, or numbers to wage war. . . . Any attempt to destroy life and property, without an objective of conquest, is a *criminal* act, and its perpetrators merit prosecution under criminal statutes. But such an attempt is not an act of war except in a loose, metaphorical sense. . . . When the word *war* is taken to justify the arbitrary exercise of power in the absence of war, metaphorical language may become an instrument of tyranny.

On paper, these distinctions seem trite, but they bespeak real and perilous differences—differences for which a serious monk admonished all who would fight to calculate the odds and consequences with a bookkeeper's punctiliousness, and then engage heart and soul. Long before Sun Tzu was a baby and no doubt well into the future, nations will get their dander up over matters that mystify subsequent generations.

Sun Tzu reminds us that empires, in the Orient or Occident, are lost when inadequate men become leaders and wage war for base reasons or no reason at all. Western history is rife with apt examples: England lost its American colonies because of the fizzle-headed King George III and his tax men; the disaster that was World War I owed much to the folly of aristocrats bent on trying out new weapons; even the Crusades resulted from arrogance and the misbegotten vanity of rulers who did no research before they attacked Palestine. The arch-conservative cartoonist David Low once quipped, "I have never met anyone who wasn't against war. Even Hitler and Mussolini were, according to themselves."

The issue of a "definite objective" is as essential to the successful military mind as its absence is to a defeated one. Sun Tzu often advises shifting points of attack to baffle the enemy and trounce him. For example, in chapter XI, paragraph 37: "By altering his arrangements and changing his plans, he keeps the enemy without definite knowledge. By shifting his camp and taking circuitous routes, he prevents the enemy from anticipating his purpose." The principle here mimics a wolf pack attacking a bear from every direction. One on one, the bear would naturally succeed against a smaller enemy, but with his energies splayed on so many fronts, he can be defeated.

Throughout the centuries, there is a deliciously romantic quality to China's intellectuals. Their passion for knowledge and for transmitting it to others is well-nigh a love affair. The genius of Sun Tzu speaks to Everyman, but his heritage speaks particularly to that belief immanent in both high Western, especially Greek, and Asian cultures—"that a coherent and logical explanation of things could be found, that the world did not ultimately rest upon the meaningless and arbitrary fiat of gods or demons" (*A Short History of the World*).

In more recent memory, readers who might want to conjure their own image of the spiritual and intellectual impetus that conceived and produced *The Art of War* might remember the photograph of a small, slender man standing alone before an advancing tank during the 1989 T'iananmen Square Uprising. He could as easily have been Sun Tzu or his descendant Sun Pin, author of a text that has come to be called *The Lost Art of War* or *The Art of War II*.

Sun Tzu's work is a unique admixture of simplicity, an utter absence of self-importance, suffused by the authority born of experience, and a breath-taking determination and passion for "ordering"—for setting the record straight, for getting out the truth, whatever that might be, whatever the consequences. In the pages that follow, you will not find the wicked delight Niccolò Machiavelli, the Renaissance Italian author of *The Prince*, took in describing the deceptions and stratagems of the profane world. *The Art of War* is quintessentially Chinese: wise beyond its pages, cryptic, simple, wonderfully profound—and at its root, pacific.

Dallas Galvin is a writer and journalist specializing in international affairs and the arts. She has reported on military affairs in Latin America and Asia and produced documentaries for the NATO Alliance.

To my brother
Captain Valentine Giles, R.C.
in the hope that
a work 2400 years old
may yet contain lessons worth consideration
by the soldier of to-day
this translation
is affectionately dedicated
—Lionel Giles

PREFACE*

by Lionel Giles

THE SEVENTH VOLUME OF "Mémoires concernant l'histoire, les sciences, les arts, les mœurs, les usages, &c., des Chinois" [Memoirs concerning the history, sciences, arts, habits, customs, etc., of the Chinese; published at Paris in 1782] is devoted to the Art of War, and contains, amongst other treatises, "Les Treize Articles de Sun-tse" [The Thirteen Articles of Sun Tzu], translated from the Chinese by a Jesuit Father, Joseph Amiot. Père Amiot appears to have enjoyed no small reputation as a sinologue in his day, and the field of his labours was certainly extensive. But his so-called translation of Sun Tzu, if placed side by side with the original, is seen at once to be little better than an imposture. It contains a great deal that Sun Tzu did not write, and very little indeed of what he did. . . .

Throughout the nineteenth century, which saw a wonderful development in the study of Chinese literature, no translator ventured to tackle Sun Tzu, although his work was known to be highly valued in China as by far the oldest and best compendium of military science. It was not until the year 1905 that the first English translation, by Captain E. F. Calthrop, R.F.A.,

*Edited from the original Preface to the 1910 Luzac & Co. edition.

appeared at Tokyo under the title "Sonshi" (the Japanese form of Sun Tzu). Unfortunately, it was evident that the translator's knowledge of Chinese was far too scanty to fit him to grapple with the manifold difficulties of Sun Tzu. He himself acknowledges that without the aid of two Japanese gentlemen "the accompanying translation would have been impossible." We can only wonder, then, that with their help it should have been so excessively bad. It is not merely a question of downright blunders. . . . Omissions were frequent; hard passages were wilfully distorted or slurred over. . . .

From blemishes of this nature, at least, I believe that the present translation is free. It was not undertaken out of any inflated estimate of my own powers; but I could not help feeling that Sun Tzu deserved a better fate than had befallen him, and I knew that, at any rate, I could hardly fail to improve on the work of my predecessors. . . .

A few special features of the present volume may now be noticed. In the first place, the text has been cut up into numbered paragraphs, both in order to facilitate cross-reference and for the convenience of students generally. The division follows broadly that of Sun Hsing-yen's edition, but I have sometimes found it desirable to join two or more of his paragraphs into one. [A] . . . feature borrowed from "The Chinese Classics" is the printing of text, translation and notes on the same page; the notes, however, are inserted, according to the Chinese method, immediately after the passages to which they refer. From the mass of native [Chinese] commentary my aim has been to extract the cream only. . . . Though constituting in itself an important branch of Chinese literature, very little commentary of this kind has hitherto been made directly accessible by translation.

THE
ART OF WAR

CONTENTS

Sun Tzu on
The Art of War

I.

LAYING PLANS

1. Sun Tzu said: The art of war is of vital importance to the State.

2. It is a matter of life and death, a road either to safety or to ruin. Hence it is a subject of inquiry which can on no account be neglected.

3. The art of war, then, is governed by five constant factors, to be taken into account in one's deliberations, when seeking to determine the conditions obtaining in the field.

4. These are: (1) The Moral Law; (2) Heaven; (3) Earth; (4) The Commander; (5) Method and discipline.

5, 6. *The Moral Law* causes the people to be in complete accord with their ruler, so that they will follow him regardless of their lives, undismayed by any danger.

7. *Heaven* signifies night and day, cold and heat, times and seasons.

8. *Earth* comprises distances, great and small; danger and security; open ground and narrow passes; the chances of life and death.

9. *The Commander* stands for the virtues of wisdom, sincerity, benevolence, courage and strictness.

10. By *Method and discipline* are to be understood the marshalling of the army in its proper subdivisions, the gradations of rank among the officers, the maintenance of roads by which supplies may reach the army, and the control of military expenditure.

11. These five heads should be familiar to every general: he who knows them will be victorious; he who knows them not will fail.

12. Therefore, in your deliberations, when seeking to determine the military conditions, let them be made the basis of a comparison, in this wise:

13. (1) Which of the two sovereigns is imbued with the Moral Law?
(2) Which of the two generals has most ability?
(3) With whom lie the advantages derived from Heaven and Earth?
(4) On which side is discipline most rigorously enforced?
(5) Which army is the stronger?
(6) On which side are officers and men more highly trained?
(7) In which army is there the greater constancy both in reward and punishment?

14. By means of these seven considerations I can forecast victory or defeat.

15. The general that hearkens to my counsel and acts upon it, will conquer:—let such a one be retained in command! The general that hearkens not to my counsel nor acts upon it, will suffer defeat:—let such a one be dismissed!

16. While heeding the profit of my counsel, avail yourself also of any helpful circumstances over and beyond the ordinary rules.

17. According as circumstances are favourable, one should modify one's plans.

18. All warfare is based on deception.

19. Hence, when able to attack, we must seem unable; when using our forces, we must seem inactive; when we are near, we must make the enemy believe we are far away; when far away, we must make him believe we are near.

20. Hold out baits to entice the enemy. Feign disorder, and crush him.

21. If he is secure at all points, be prepared for him. If he is in superior strength, evade him.

22. If your opponent is of choleric temper, seek to irritate him. Pretend to be weak, that he may grow arrogant.

23. If he is taking his ease, give him no rest.

24. Attack him where he is unprepared, appear where you are not expected.

25. These military devices, leading to victory, must not be divulged beforehand.

26. Now the general who wins a battle makes many calculations in his temple ere the battle is fought. The general who loses a battle makes but few calculations beforehand. Thus do many calculations lead to victory, and few calculations to defeat: how much more no calculation at all! It is by attention to this point that I can foresee who is likely to win or lose.

作戰 篇

II.

WAGING WAR

———— ✐ ————

1. Sun Tzu said: In the operations of war, where there are in the field a thousand swift chariots, as many heavy chariots, and a hundred thousand mail-clad soldiers, with provisions enough to carry them a thousand *li*, the expenditure at home and at the front, including entertainment of guests, small items such as glue and paint, and sums spent on chariots and armour, will reach the total of a thousand ounces of silver per day. Such is the cost of raising an army of 100,000 men.

2. When you engage in actual fighting, if victory is long in coming, the men's weapons will grow dull and their ardour will be damped. If you lay siege to a town, you will exhaust your strength.

3. Again, if the campaign is protracted, the resources of the State will not be equal to the strain.

4. Now, when your weapons are dulled, your ardour damped, your strength exhausted and your treasure spent, other chieftains will spring up to take advantage of your extremity. Then no man, however wise, will be able to avert the consequences that must ensue.

5. Thus, though we have heard of stupid haste in war, cleverness has never been seen associated with long delays.

6. There is no instance of a country having benefited from prolonged warfare.

7. It is only one who is thoroughly acquainted with the evils of war that can thoroughly understand the profitable way of carrying it on.

8. The skilful soldier does not raise a second levy, neither are his supply-wagons loaded more than twice.

9. Bring war material with you from home, but forage on the enemy. Thus the army will have food enough for its needs.

10. Poverty of the State exchequer causes an army to be maintained by contributions from a distance. Contributing to maintain an army at a distance causes the people to be impoverished.

11. On the other hand, the proximity of an army causes prices to go up, and high prices cause the people's substance to be drained away.

12. When their substance is drained away, the peasantry will be afflicted by heavy exactions.

13, 14. With this loss of substance and exhaustion of strength, the homes of the people will be stripped bare, and three-tenths of their incomes will be dissipated; while Government expenses for broken chariots, worn-out horses, breast-plates and helmets, bows and arrows, spears and shields, protective mantlets, draught-oxen and heavy waggons, will amount to four-tenths of its total revenue.

15. Hence a wise general makes a point of foraging on the enemy. One carload of the enemy's provisions is equivalent to twenty of one's own, and likewise a single *picul* of his provender is equivalent to twenty from one's own store.

16. Now in order to kill the enemy, our men must be roused to anger; that there may be advantage from defeating the enemy, they must have their rewards.

17. Therefore in chariot fighting, when ten or more chariots have been taken, those should be rewarded who took the first. Our own flags should be substituted for those of the enemy, and the chariots mingled and used in conjunction with ours. The captured soldiers should be kindly treated and kept.

18. This is called, using the conquered foe to augment one's own strength.

19. In war, then, let your great object be victory, not lengthy campaigns.

20. Thus it may be known that the leader of armies is the arbiter of the people's fate, the man on whom it depends whether the nation shall be in peace or in peril.

謀攻篇

III.

ATTACK BY STRATAGEM

———— ✑ ————

1. Sun Tzu said: In the practical art of war, the best thing of all is to take the enemy's country whole and intact; to shatter and destroy it is not so good. So, too, it is better to capture an army entire than to destroy it, to capture a regiment, a detachment or a company entire than to destroy them.

2. Hence to fight and conquer in all your battles is not supreme excellence; supreme excellence consists in breaking the enemy's resistance without fighting.

3. Thus the highest form of generalship is to baulk the enemy's plans; the next best is to prevent the junction of the enemy's forces; the next in order is to attack the enemy's army in the field; and the worst policy of all is to besiege walled cities.

4. The rule is, not to besiege walled cities if it can possibly be avoided. The preparation of mantlets, movable shelters, and various implements of war, will take up three whole months; and the piling up of mounds over against the walls will take three months more.

5. The general, unable to control his irritation, will launch his men to the assault like swarming ants, with the result that one-third of his men are slain, while the town still remains untaken. Such are the disastrous effects of a siege.

6. Therefore the skilful leader subdues the enemy's troops without any fighting; he captures their cities without laying siege to them; he overthrows their kingdom without lengthy operations in the field.

7. With his forces intact he will dispute the mastery of the Empire, and thus, without losing a man, his triumph will be complete. This is the method of attacking by stratagem.

8. It is the rule in war, if our forces are ten to the enemy's one, to surround him; if five to one, to attack him; if twice as numerous, to divide our army into two.

9. If equally matched, we can offer battle; if slightly inferior in numbers, we can avoid the enemy; if quite unequal in every way, we can flee from him.

10. Hence, though an obstinate fight may be made by a small force, in the end it must be captured by the larger force.

11. Now the general is the bulwark of the State: if the bulwark is complete at all points, the State will be strong; if the bulwark is defective, the State will be weak.

12. There are three ways in which a ruler can bring misfortune upon his army:—

13. (1) By commanding the army to advance or to retreat, being ignorant of the fact that it cannot obey. This is called hobbling the army.

14. (2) By attempting to govern an army in the same way as he administers a kingdom, being ignorant of the conditions which obtain in an army. This causes restlessness in the soldiers' minds.

15. (3) By employing the officers of his army without discrimination, through ignorance of the military principle of adaptation to circumstances. This shakes the confidence of the soldiers.

16. But when the army is restless and distrustful, trouble is sure to come from the other feudal princes. This is simply bringing anarchy into the army, and flinging victory away.

17. Thus we may know that there are five essentials for victory:

(1) He will win who knows when to fight and when not to fight.

(2) He will win who knows how to handle both superior and inferior forces.

(3) He will win whose army is animated by the same spirit throughout all its ranks.

(4) He will win who, prepared himself, waits to take the enemy unprepared.

(5) He will win who has military capacity and is not interfered with by the sovereign.

Victory lies in the knowledge of these five points.

18. Hence the saying: If you know the enemy and know yourself, you need not fear the result of a hundred battles. If you know yourself but not the enemy, for every victory gained you will also suffer a defeat. If you know neither the enemy nor yourself, you will succumb in every battle.

形 篇

IV.
TACTICAL DISPOSITIONS

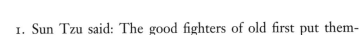

1. Sun Tzu said: The good fighters of old first put themselves beyond the possibility of defeat, and then waited for an opportunity of defeating the enemy.

2. To secure ourselves against defeat lies in our own hands, but the opportunity of defeating the enemy is provided by the enemy himself.

3. Thus the good fighter is able to secure himself against defeat, but cannot make certain of defeating the enemy.

4. Hence the saying: One may *know* how to conquer without being able to *do* it.

5. Security against defeat implies defensive tactics; ability to defeat the enemy means taking the offensive.

6. Standing on the defensive indicates insufficient strength; attacking, a superabundance of strength.

7. The general who is skilled in defence hides in the most secret recesses of the earth; he who is skilled in attack flashes forth from the topmost heights of heaven. Thus on the one hand we have ability to protect ourselves; on the other, a victory that is complete.

8. To see victory only when it is within the ken of the common herd is not the acme of excellence.

9. Neither is it the acme of excellence if you fight and conquer and the whole Empire says, "Well done!"

10. To lift an autumn hair is no sign of great strength; to see sun and moon is no sign of sharp sight; to hear the noise of thunder is no sign of a quick ear.

11. What the ancients called a clever fighter is one who not only wins, but excels in winning with ease.

12. Hence his victories bring him neither reputation for wisdom nor credit for courage.

13. He wins his battles by making no mistakes. Making no mistakes is what establishes the certainty of victory, for it means conquering an enemy that is already defeated.

14. Hence the skilful fighter puts himself into a position which makes defeat impossible, and does not miss the moment for defeating the enemy.

15. Thus it is that in war the victorious strategist only seeks battle after the victory has been won, whereas he who is destined to defeat first fights and afterwards looks for victory.

16. The consummate leader cultivates the moral law, and strictly adheres to method and discipline; thus it is in his power to control success.

17. In respect of military method, we have, firstly, Measurement; secondly, Estimation of quantity; thirdly, Calculation; fourthly, Balancing of chances; fifthly, Victory.

18. Measurement owes its existence to Earth; Estimation of quantity to Measurement; Calculation to Estimation of quantity; Balancing of chances to Calculation; and Victory to Balancing of chances.

19. A victorious army opposed to a routed one, is as a pound's weight placed in the scale against a single grain.

20. The onrush of a conquering force is like the bursting of pent-up waters into a chasm a thousand fathoms deep. So much for tactical dispositions.

執篇

V.

ENERGY

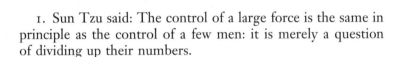

1. Sun Tzu said: The control of a large force is the same in principle as the control of a few men: it is merely a question of dividing up their numbers.

2. Fighting with a large army under your command is no-wise different from fighting with a small one: it is merely a question of instituting signs and signals.

3. To ensure that your whole host may withstand the brunt of the enemy's attack and remain unshaken—this is effected by manœuvres direct and indirect.

4. That the impact of your army may be like a grindstone dashed against an egg—this is effected by the science of weak points and strong.

5. In all fighting, the direct method may be used for joining battle, but indirect methods will be needed in order to secure victory.

6. Indirect tactics, efficiently applied, are inexhaustible as Heaven and Earth, unending as the flow of rivers and streams; like the sun and moon, they end but to begin anew; like the four seasons, they pass away but to return once more.

7. There are not more than five musical notes, yet the combinations of these five give rise to more melodies than can ever be heard.

8. There are not more than five primary colours, yet in combination they produce more hues than can ever be seen.

9. There are not more than five cardinal tastes, yet combinations of them yield more flavours than can ever be tasted.

10. In battle, there are not more than two methods of attack—the direct and the indirect; yet these two in combination give rise to an endless series of manœuvers.

11. The direct and the indirect lead on to each other in turn. It is like moving in a circle—you never come to an end. Who can exhaust the possibilities of their combination?

12. The onset of troops is like the rush of a torrent which will even roll stones along in its course.

13. The quality of decision is like the well-timed swoop of a falcon which enables it to strike and destroy its victim.

14. Therefore the good fighter will be terrible in his onset, and prompt in his decision.

15. Energy may be likened to the bending of a crossbow; decision, to the releasing of the trigger.

16. Amid the turmoil and tumult of battle, there may be seeming disorder and yet no real disorder at all; amid confusion and chaos, your array may be without head or tail, yet it will be proof against defeat.

17. Simulated disorder postulates perfect discipline; simulated fear postulates courage; simulated weakness postulates strength.

18. Hiding order beneath the cloak of disorder is simply a question of subdivision; concealing courage under a show of

timidity presupposes a fund of latent energy; masking strength with weakness is to be effected by tactical dispositions.

19. Thus one who is skilful at keeping the enemy on the move maintains deceitful appearances, according to which the enemy will act. He sacrifices something, that the enemy may snatch at it.

20. By holding out baits, he keeps him on the march; then with a body of picked men he lies in wait for him.

21. The clever combatant looks to the effect of combined energy, and does not require too much from individuals. Hence his ability to pick out the right men and to utilise combined energy.

22. When he utilises combined energy, his fighting men become as it were like unto rolling logs or stones. For it is the nature of a log or stone to remain motionless on level ground, and to move when on a slope; if four-cornered, to come to a standstill, but if round-shaped, to go rolling down.

23. Thus the energy developed by good fighting men is as the momentum of a round stone rolled down a mountain thousands of feet in height. So much on the subject of energy.

虛實篇

VI.

WEAK POINTS AND
STRONG

1. Sun Tzu said: Whoever is first in the field and awaits the coming of the enemy, will be fresh for the fight; whoever is second in the field and has to hasten to battle, will arrive exhausted.

2. Therefore the clever combatant imposes his will on the enemy, but does not allow the enemy's will to be imposed upon him.

3. By holding out advantages to him, he can cause the enemy to approach of his own accord; or, by inflicting damage, he can make it impossible for the enemy to draw near.

4. If the enemy is taking his ease, he can harass him; if well supplied with food, he can starve him out; if quietly encamped, he can force him to move.

5. Appear at points which the enemy must hasten to defend; march swiftly to places where you are not expected.

6. An army may march great distances without distress, if it marches through country where the enemy is not.

7. You can be sure of succeeding in your attacks if you only attack places which are undefended. You can ensure the safety of your defence if you only hold positions that cannot be attacked.

8. Hence that general is skilful in attack whose opponent does not know what to defend; and he is skilful in defence whose opponent does not know what to attack.

9. O divine art of subtlety and secrecy! Through you we learn to be invisible, through you inaudible; and hence we can hold the enemy's fate in our hands.

10. You may advance and be absolutely irresistible, if you make for the enemy's weak points; you may retire and be safe from pursuit if your movements are more rapid than those of the enemy.

11. If we wish to fight, the enemy can be forced to an engagement even though he be sheltered behind a high rampart and a deep ditch. All we need do is to attack some other place that he will be obliged to relieve.

12. If we do not wish to fight, we can prevent the enemy from engaging us even though the lines of our encampment be merely traced out on the ground. All we need do is to throw something odd and unaccountable in his way.

13. By discovering the enemy's dispositions and remaining invisible ourselves, we can keep our forces concentrated, while the enemy's must be divided.

14. We can form a single united body, while the enemy must split up into fractions. Hence there will be a whole pitted against separate parts of a whole, which means that we shall be many to the enemy's few.

15. And if we are able thus to attack an inferior force with a superior one, our opponents will be in dire straits.

16. The spot where we intend to fight must not be made known; for then the enemy will have to prepare against a possible attack at several different points; and his forces being thus distributed in many directions, the numbers we shall have to face at any given point will be proportionately few.

17. For should the enemy strengthen his van, he will weaken his rear; should he strengthen his rear, he will weaken his van; should he strengthen his left, he will weaken his right; should he strengthen his right, he will weaken his left. If he sends reinforcements everywhere, he will everywhere be weak.

18. Numerical weakness comes from having to prepare against possible attacks; numerical strength, from compelling our adversary to make these preparations against us.

19. Knowing the place and the time of the coming battle, we may concentrate from the greatest distances in order to fight.

20. But if neither time nor place be known, then the left wing will be impotent to succour the right, the right equally impotent to succour the left, the van unable to relieve the rear, or the rear to support the van. How much more so if the furthest portions of the army are anything under a hundred *li* apart, and even the nearest are separated by several *li*!

21. Though according to my estimate the soldiers of Yüeh exceed our own in number, that shall advantage them nothing in the matter of victory. I say then that victory can be achieved.

22. Though the enemy be stronger in numbers, we may prevent him from fighting. Scheme so as to discover his plans and the likelihood of their success.

23. Rouse him, and learn the principle of his activity or inactivity. Force him to reveal himself, so as to find out his vulnerable spots.

24. Carefully compare the opposing army with your own, so that you may know where strength is superabundant and where it is deficient.

25. In making tactical dispositions, the highest pitch you can attain is to conceal them; conceal your dispositions, and you will be safe from the prying of the subtlest spies, from the machinations of the wisest brains.

26. How victory may be produced for them out of the enemy's own tactics—that is what the multitude cannot comprehend.

27. All men can see the tactics whereby I conquer, but what none can see is the strategy out of which victory is evolved.

28. Do not repeat the tactics which have gained you one victory, but let your methods be regulated by the infinite variety of circumstances.

29. Military tactics are like unto water; for water in its natural course runs away from high places and hastens downwards.

30. So in war, the way is to avoid what is strong and to strike at what is weak.

31. Water shapes its course according to the nature of the ground over which it flows; the soldier works out his victory in relation to the foe whom he is facing.

32. Therefore, just as water retains no constant shape, so in warfare there are no constant conditions.

33. He who can modify his tactics in relation to his opponent and thereby succeed in winning, may be called a heaven-born captain.

34. The five elements are not always equally predominant; the four seasons make way for each other in turn. There are short days and long; the moon has its periods of waning and waxing.

軍 爭 篇

VII.

MANŒUVRING

———

1. Sun Tzu said: In war, the general receives his commands from the sovereign.

2. Having collected an army and concentrated his forces, he must blend and harmonise the different elements thereof before pitching his camp.

3. After that, comes tactical manœuvring, than which there is nothing more difficult. The difficulty of tactical manœuvring consists in turning the devious into the direct, and misfortune into gain.

4. Thus, to take a long and circuitous route, after enticing the enemy out of the way, and though starting after him, to contrive to reach the goal before him, shows knowledge of the artifice of *deviation*.

5. Manœuvring with an army is advantageous; with an undisciplined multitude, most dangerous.

6. If you set a fully equipped army in march in order to snatch an advantage, the chances are that you will be too late. On the other hand, to detach a flying column for the purpose involves the sacrifice of its baggage and stores.

7. Thus, if you order your men to roll up their buff-coats, and make forced marches without halting day or night, covering double the usual distance at a stretch, doing a hundred *li* in order to wrest an advantage, the leaders of all your three divisions will fall into the hands of the enemy.

8. The stronger men will be in front, the jaded ones will fall behind, and on this plan only one-tenth of your army will reach its destination.

9. If you march fifty *li* in order to outmanœuvre the enemy, you will lose the leader of your first division, and only half your force will reach the goal.

10. If you march thirty *li* with the same object, two-thirds of your army will arrive.

11. We may take it then that an army without its baggage-train is lost; without provisions it is lost; without bases of supply it is lost.

12. We cannot enter into alliances until we are acquainted with the designs of our neighbours.

13. We are not fit to lead an army on the march unless we are familiar with the face of the country—its mountains and forests, its pitfalls and precipices, its marshes and swamps.

14. We shall be unable to turn natural advantages to account unless we make use of local guides.

15. In war, practise dissimulation, and you will succeed. Move only if there is a real advantage to be gained.

16. Whether to concentrate or to divide your troops, must be decided by circumstances.

17. Let your rapidity be that of the wind, your compactness that of the forest.

18. In raiding and plundering be like fire, in immovability like a mountain.

19. Let your plans be dark and impenetrable as night, and when you move, fall like a thunderbolt.

20. When you plunder a countryside, let the spoil be divided amongst your men; when you capture new territory, cut it up into allotments for the benefit of the soldiery.

21. Ponder and deliberate before you make a move.

22. He will conquer who has learnt the artifice of deviation. Such is the art of manœuvring.

23. The Book of Army Management says: On the field of battle, the spoken word does not carry far enough: hence the institution of gongs and drums. Nor can ordinary objects be seen clearly enough: hence the institution of banners and flags.

24. Gongs and drums, banners and flags, are means whereby the ears and eyes of the host may be focused on one particular point.

25. The host thus forming a single united body, it is impossible either for the brave to advance alone, or for the cowardly to retreat alone. This is the art of handling large masses of men.

26. In night-fighting, then, make much use of signal-fires and drums, and in fighting by day, of flags and banners, as a means of influencing the ears and eyes of your army.

27. A whole army may be robbed of its spirit; a commander-in-chief may be robbed of his presence of mind.

28. Now a soldier's spirit is keenest in the morning; by noonday it has begun to flag; and in the evening, his mind is bent only on returning to camp.

29. A clever general, therefore, avoids an army when its spirit is keen, but attacks it when it is sluggish and inclined to return. This is the art of studying moods.

30. Disciplined and calm, to await the appearance of disorder and hubbub amongst the enemy:—this is the art of retaining self-possession.

31. To be near the goal while the enemy is still far from it, to wait at ease while the enemy is toiling and struggling, to be well-fed while the enemy is famished:—this is the art of husbanding one's strength.

32. To refrain from intercepting an enemy whose banners are in perfect order, to refrain from attacking an army drawn up in calm and confident array:—this is the art of studying circumstances.

33. It is a military axiom not to advance uphill against the enemy, nor to oppose him when he comes downhill.

34. Do not pursue an enemy who simulates flight; do not attack soldiers whose temper is keen.

35. Do not swallow a bait offered by the enemy. Do not interfere with an army that is returning home.

36. When you surround an army, leave an outlet free. Do not press a desperate foe too hard.

37. Such is the art of warfare.

九 變 篇

VIII.
VARIATION OF TACTICS

———— ❧ ————

1. Sun Tzu said: In war, the general receives his commands from the sovereign, collects his army and concentrates his forces.

2. When in difficult country, do not encamp. In country where high roads intersect, join hands with your allies. Do not linger in dangerously isolated positions. In hemmed-in situations, you must resort to stratagem. In a desperate position, you must fight.

3. There are roads which must not be followed, armies which must not be attacked, towns which must not be besieged, positions which must not be contested, commands of the sovereign which must not be obeyed.

4. The general who thoroughly understands the advantages that accompany variation of tactics knows how to handle his troops.

5. The general who does not understand these, may be well acquainted with the configuration of the country, yet he will not be able to turn his knowledge to practical account.

6. So, the student of war who is unversed in the art of varying his plans, even though he be acquainted with the Five Advantages, will fail to make the best use of his men.

7. Hence in the wise leader's plans, considerations of advantage and of disadvantage will be blended together.

8. If our expectation of advantage be tempered in this way, we may succeed in accomplishing the essential part of our schemes.

9. If, on the other hand, in the midst of difficulties we are always ready to seize an advantage, we may extricate ourselves from misfortune.

10. Reduce the hostile chiefs by inflicting damage on them; make trouble for them, and keep them constantly engaged; hold out specious allurements, and make them rush to any given point.

11. The art of war teaches us to rely not on the likelihood of the enemy's not coming, but on our own readiness to receive him; not on the chance of his not attacking, but rather on the fact that we have made our position unassailable.

12. There are five dangerous faults which may affect a general: (1) Recklessness, which leads to destruction; (2) cowardice, which leads to capture; (3) a hasty temper, which can be provoked by insults; (4) a delicacy of honour which is sensitive to shame; (5) over-solicitude for his men, which exposes him to worry and trouble.

13. These are the five besetting sins of a general, ruinous to the conduct of war.

14. When an army is overthrown and its leader slain, the cause will surely be found among these five dangerous faults. Let them be a subject of meditation.

行軍篇

IX.

THE ARMY
ON THE MARCH

————⟨⟩————

1. Sun Tzu said: We come now to the question of encamping the army, and observing signs of the enemy. Pass quickly over mountains, and keep in the neighbourhood of valleys.

2. Camp in high places, facing the sun. Do not climb heights in order to fight. So much for mountain warfare.

3. After crossing a river, you should get far away from it.

4. When an invading force crosses a river in its onward march, do not advance to meet it in mid-stream. It will be best to let half the army get across, and then deliver your attack.

5. If you are anxious to fight, you should not go to meet the invader near a river which he has to cross.

6. Moor your craft higher up than the enemy, and facing the sun. Do not move up-stream to meet the enemy. So much for river warfare.

7. In crossing salt-marshes, your sole concern should be to get over them quickly, without any delay.

8. If forced to fight in a salt-marsh, you should have water and grass near you, and get your back to a clump of trees. So much for operations in salt-marshes.

9. In dry, level country, take up an easily accessible position with rising ground to your right and on your rear, so that the danger may be in front, and safety lie behind. So much for campaigning in flat country.

10. These are the four useful branches of military knowledge which enabled the Yellow Emperor to vanquish four several sovereigns.

11. All armies prefer high ground to low, and sunny places to dark.

12. If you are careful of your men, and camp on hard ground, the army will be free from disease of every kind, and this will spell victory.

13. When you come to a hill or a bank, occupy the sunny side, with the slope on your right rear. Thus you will at once act for the benefit of your soldiers and utilise the natural advantages of the ground.

14. When, in consequence of heavy rains up-country, a river which you wish to ford is swollen and flecked with foam, you must wait until it subsides.

15. Country in which there are precipitous cliffs with torrents running between, deep natural hollows, confined places, tangled thickets, quagmires and crevasses, should be left with all possible speed and not approached.

16. While we keep away from such places, we should get the enemy to approach them; while we face them, we should let the enemy have them on his rear.

17. If in the neighbourhood of your camp there should be any hilly country, ponds surrounded by aquatic grass, hollow basins filled with reeds, or woods with thick undergrowth, they

must be carefully routed out and searched; for these are places where men in ambush or insidious spies are likely to be lurking.

18. When the enemy is close at hand and remains quiet, he is relying on the natural strength of his position.

19. When he keeps aloof and tries to provoke a battle, he is anxious for the other side to advance.

20. If his place of encampment is easy of access, he is tendering a bait.

21. Movement amongst the trees of a forest shows that the enemy is advancing. The appearance of a number of screens in the midst of thick grass means that the enemy wants to make us suspicious.

22. The rising of birds in their flight is the sign of an ambuscade. Startled beasts indicate that a sudden attack is coming.

23. When there is dust rising in a high column, it is the sign of chariots advancing; when the dust is low, but spread over a wide area, it betokens the approach of infantry. When it branches out in different directions, it shows that parties have been sent to collect firewood. A few clouds of dust moving to and fro signify that the army is encamping.

24. Humble words and increased preparations are signs that the enemy is about to advance. Violent language and driving forward as if to the attack are signs that he will retreat.

25. When the light chariots come out first and take up a position on the wings, it is a sign that the enemy is forming for battle.

26. Peace proposals unaccompanied by a sworn covenant indicate a plot.

27. When there is much running about and the soldiers fall into rank, it means that the critical moment has come.

28. When some are seen advancing and some retreating, it is a lure.

29. When the soldiers stand leaning on their spears, they are faint from want of food.

30. If those who are sent to draw water begin by drinking themselves, the army is suffering from thirst.

31. If the enemy sees an advantage to be gained and makes no effort to secure it, the soldiers are exhausted.

32. If birds gather on any spot, it is unoccupied. Clamour by night betokens nervousness.

33. If there is disturbance in the camp, the general's authority is weak. If the banners and flags are shifted about, sedition is afoot. If the officers are angry, it means that the men are weary.

34. When an army feeds its horses with grain and kills its cattle for food, and when the men do not hang their cooking-pots over the camp-fires, showing that they will not return to their tents, you may know that they are determined to fight to the death.

35. The sight of men whispering together in small knots or speaking in subdued tones points to disaffection amongst the rank and file.

36. Too frequent rewards signify that the enemy is at the end of his resources; too many punishments betray a condition of dire distress.

37. To begin by bluster, but afterwards to take fright at the enemy's numbers, shows a supreme lack of intelligence.

38. When envoys are sent with compliments in their mouths, it is a sign that the enemy wishes for a truce.

39. If the enemy's troops march up angrily and remain facing ours for a long time without either joining battle or taking themselves off again, the situation is one that demands great vigilance and circumspection.

40. If our troops are no more in number than the enemy, that is amply sufficient; it only means that no direct attack can be made. What we can do is simply to concentrate all our available strength, keep a close watch on the enemy, and obtain reinforcements.

41. He who exercises no forethought but makes light of his opponents is sure to be captured by them.

42. If soldiers are punished before they have grown attached to you, they will not prove submissive; and, unless submissive, they will be practically useless. If, when the soldiers have become attached to you, punishments are not enforced, they will still be useless.

43. Therefore soldiers must be treated in the first instance with humanity, but kept under control by means of iron discipline. This is a certain road to victory.

44. If in training soldiers commands are habitually enforced, the army will be well-disciplined; if not, its discipline will be bad.

45. If a general shows confidence in his men but always insists on his orders being obeyed, the gain will be mutual.

地形篇

X.

TERRAIN

1. Sun Tzu said: We may distinguish six kinds of terrain, to wit: (1) Accessible ground; (2) entangling ground; (3) temporising ground; (4) narrow passes; (5) precipitous heights; (6) positions at a great distance from the enemy.

2. Ground which can be freely traversed by both sides is called *accessible*.

3. With regard to ground of this nature, be before the enemy in occupying the raised and sunny spots, and carefully guard your line of supplies. Then you will be able to fight with advantage.

4. Ground which can be abandoned but is hard to re-occupy is called *entangling*.

5. From a position of this sort, if the enemy is unprepared, you may sally forth and defeat him. But if the enemy is prepared for your coming, and you fail to defeat him, then, return being impossible, disaster will ensue.

6. When the position is such that neither side will gain by making the first move, it is called *temporising* ground.

7. In a position of this sort, even though the enemy should offer us an attractive bait, it will be advisable not to stir forth,

but rather to retreat, thus enticing the enemy in his turn; then, when part of his army has come out, we may deliver our attack with advantage.

8. With regard to *narrow passes*, if you can occupy them first, let them be strongly garrisoned and await the advent of the enemy.

9. Should the enemy forestall you in occupying a pass, do not go after him if the pass is fully garrisoned, but only if it is weakly garrisoned.

10. With regard to *precipitous heights*, if you are beforehand with your adversary, you should occupy the raised and sunny spots, and there wait for him to come up.

11. If the enemy has occupied them before you, do not follow him, but retreat and try to entice him away.

12. If you are situated at a great distance from the enemy, and the strength of the two armies is equal, it is not easy to provoke a battle, and fighting will be to your disadvantage.

13. These six are the principles connected with Earth. The general who has attained a responsible post must be careful to study them.

14. Now an army is exposed to six several calamities, not arising from natural causes, but from faults for which the general is responsible. These are: (1) Flight; (2) insubordination; (3) collapse; (4) ruin; (5) disorganisation; (6) rout.

15. Other conditions being equal, if one force is hurled against another ten times its size, the result will be the *flight* of the former.

16. When the common soldiers are too strong and their officers too weak, the result is *insubordination*. When the officers are too strong and the common soldiers too weak, the result is *collapse*.

17. When the higher officers are angry and insubordinate, and on meeting the enemy give battle on their own account from a feeling of resentment, before the commander-in-chief can tell whether or no he is in a position to fight, the result is *ruin*.

18. When the general is weak and without authority; when his orders are not clear and distinct; when there are no fixed duties assigned to officers and men, and the ranks are formed in a slovenly haphazard manner, the result is utter *disorganisation*.

19. When a general, unable to estimate the enemy's strength, allows an inferior force to engage a larger one, or hurls a weak detachment against a powerful one, and neglects to place picked soldiers in the front rank, the result must be a *rout*.

20. These are six ways of courting defeat, which must be carefully noted by the general who has attained a responsible post.

21. The natural formation of the country is the soldier's best ally; but a power of estimating the adversary, of controlling the forces of victory, and of shrewdly calculating difficulties, dangers and distances, constitutes the test of a great general.

22. He who knows these things, and in fighting puts his knowledge into practice, will win his battles. He who knows them not, nor practises them, will surely be defeated.

23. If fighting is sure to result in victory, then you must fight, even though the ruler forbid it; if fighting will not result in victory, then you must not fight even at the ruler's bidding.

24. The general who advances without coveting fame and retreats without fearing disgrace, whose only thought is to protect his country and do good service for his sovereign, is the jewel of the kingdom.

25. Regard your soldiers as your children, and they will follow you into the deepest valleys; look on them as your own beloved sons, and they will stand by you even unto death.

26. If, however, you are indulgent, but unable to make your authority felt; kind-hearted, but unable to enforce your commands; and incapable, moreover, of quelling disorder: then your soldiers must be likened to spoilt children; they are useless for any practical purpose.

27. If we know that our own men are in a condition to attack, but are unaware that the enemy is not open to attack, we have gone only halfway towards victory.

28. If we know that the enemy is open to attack, but are unaware that our own men are not in a condition to attack, we have gone only halfway towards victory.

29. If we know that the enemy is open to attack, and also know that our men are in a condition to attack, but are unaware that the nature of the ground makes fighting impracticable, we have still gone only halfway towards victory.

30. Hence the experienced soldier, once in motion, is never bewildered; once he has broken camp, he is never at a loss.

31. Hence the saying: If you know the enemy and know yourself, your victory will not stand in doubt; if you know Heaven and know Earth, you may make your victory complete.

九 地 篇

XI.

THE NINE SITUATIONS

⟶ ⫘ ⟶

1. Sun Tzu said: The art of war recognises nine varieties of ground: (1) Dispersive ground; (2) facile ground; (3) contentious ground; (4) open ground; (5) ground of intersecting highways; (6) serious ground; (7) difficult ground; (8) hemmed-in ground; (9) desperate ground.

2. When a chieftain is fighting in his own territory, it is dispersive ground.

3. When he has penetrated into hostile territory, but to no great distance, it is facile ground.

4. Ground the possession of which imports great advantage to either side, is contentious ground.

5. Ground on which each side has liberty of movement is open ground.

6. Ground which forms the key to three contiguous states, so that he who occupies it first has most of the Empire at his command, is ground of intersecting highways.

7. When an army has penetrated into the heart of a hostile country, leaving a number of fortified cities in its rear, it is serious ground.

8. Mountain forests, rugged steeps, marshes and fens—all country that is hard to traverse: this is difficult ground.

9. Ground which is reached through narrow gorges, and from which we can only retire by tortuous paths, so that a small number of the enemy would suffice to crush a large body of our men: this is hemmed-in ground.

10. Ground on which we can only be saved from destruction by fighting without delay, is desperate ground.

11. On dispersive ground, therefore, fight not. On facile ground, halt not. On contentious ground, attack not.

12. On open ground, do not try to block the enemy's way. On ground of intersecting highways, join hands with your allies.

13. On serious ground, gather in plunder. In difficult ground, keep steadily on the march.

14. On hemmed-in ground, resort to stratagem. On desperate ground, fight.

15. Those who were called skilful leaders of old knew how to drive a wedge between the enemy's front and rear; to prevent co-operation between his large and small divisions; to hinder the good troops from rescuing the bad, the officers from rallying their men.

16. When the enemy's men were scattered, they prevented them from concentrating; even when their forces were united, they managed to keep them in disorder.

17. When it was to their advantage, they made a forward move; when otherwise, they stopped still.

18. If asked how to cope with a great host of the enemy in orderly array and on the point of marching to the attack, I should say: "Begin by seizing something which your opponent holds dear; then he will be amenable to your will."

19. Rapidity is the essence of war: take advantage of the enemy's unreadiness, make your way by unexpected routes, and attack unguarded spots.

20. The following are the principles to be observed by an invading force: The further you penetrate into a country, the greater will be the solidarity of your troops, and thus the defenders will not prevail against you.

21. Make forays in fertile country in order to supply your army with food.

22. Carefully study the well-being of your men, and do not overtax them. Concentrate your energy and hoard your strength. Keep your army continually on the move, and devise unfathomable plans.

23. Throw your soldiers into positions whence there is no escape, and they will prefer death to flight. If they will face death, there is nothing they may not achieve. Officers and men alike will put forth their uttermost strength.

24. Soldiers when in desperate straits lose the sense of fear. If there is no place of refuge, they will stand firm. If they are in the heart of a hostile country, they will show a stubborn front. If there is no help for it, they will fight hard.

25. Thus, without waiting to be marshalled, the soldiers will be constantly on the *qui vive*; without waiting to be asked, they will do your will; without restrictions, they will be faithful; without giving orders, they can be trusted.

26. Prohibit the taking of omens, and do away with superstitious doubts. Then, until death itself comes, no calamity need be feared.

27. If our soldiers are not overburdened with money, it is not because they have a distaste for riches; if their lives are not unduly long, it is not because they are disinclined to longevity.

28. On the day they are ordered out to battle, your soldiers may weep, those sitting up bedewing their garments, and those lying down letting the tears run down their cheeks. But let them once be brought to bay, and they will display the courage of a Chu or a Kuei.

29. The skilful tactician may be likened to the *shuai-jan*. Now the *shuai-jan* is a snake that is found in the Ch'ang mountains. Strike at its head, and you will be attacked by its tail; strike at its tail, and you will be attacked by its head; strike at its middle, and you will be attacked by head and tail both.

30. Asked if an army can be made to imitate the *shuai-jan*, I should answer, Yes. For the men of Wu and the men of Yüeh are enemies; yet if they are crossing a river in the same boat and are caught by a storm, they will come to each other's assistance just as the left hand helps the right.

31. Hence it is not enough to put one's trust in the tethering of horses, and the burying of chariot wheels in the ground.

32. The principle on which to manage an army is to set up one standard of courage which all must reach.

33. How to make the best of both strong and weak—that is a question involving the proper use of ground.

34. Thus the skilful general conducts his army just as though he were leading a single man, willy-nilly, by the hand.

35. It is the business of a general to be quiet and thus ensure secrecy; upright and just, and thus maintain order.

36. He must be able to mystify his officers and men by false reports and appearances, and thus keep them in total ignorance.

37. By altering his arrangements and changing his plans, he keeps the enemy without definite knowledge. By shifting his camp and taking circuitous routes, he prevents the enemy from anticipating his purpose.

38. At the critical moment, the leader of an army acts like one who has climbed up a height and then kicks away the ladder behind him. He carries his men deep into hostile territory before he shows his hand.

39. He burns his boats and breaks his cooking-pots; like a shepherd driving a flock of sheep, he drives his men this way and that, and none knows whither he is going.

40. To muster his host and bring it into danger:—this may be termed the business of the general.

41. The different measures suited to the nine varieties of ground; the expediency of aggressive or defensive tactics; and the fundamental laws of human nature: these are things that must most certainly be studied.

42. When invading hostile territory, the general principle is, that penetrating deeply brings cohesion; penetrating but a short way means dispersion.

43. When you leave your own country behind, and take your army across neighbouring territory, you find yourself on critical ground. When there are means of communication on all four sides, the ground is one of intersecting highways.

44. When you penetrate deeply into a country, it is serious ground. When you penetrate but a little way, it is facile ground.

45. When you have the enemy's strongholds on your rear, and narrow passes in front, it is hemmed-in ground. When there is no place of refuge at all, it is desperate ground.

46. Therefore, on dispersive ground, I would inspire my men with unity of purpose. On facile ground, I would see that there is close connection between all parts of my army.

47. On contentious ground, I would hurry up my rear.

48. On open ground, I would keep a vigilant eye on my defences. On ground of intersecting highways, I would consolidate my alliances.

49. On serious ground, I would try to ensure a continuous stream of supplies. On difficult ground, I would keep pushing on along the road.

50. On hemmed-in ground, I would block any way of retreat. On desperate ground, I would proclaim to my soldiers the hopelessness of saving their lives.

51. For it is the soldier's disposition to offer an obstinate resistance when surrounded, to fight hard when he cannot help himself, and to obey promptly when he has fallen into danger.

52. We cannot enter into alliance with neighbouring princes until we are acquainted with their designs. We are not fit to lead an army on the march unless we are familiar with the face of the country—its mountains and forests, its pitfalls and precipices, its marshes and swamps. We shall be unable to turn natural advantages to account unless we make use of local guides.

53. To be ignorant of any one of the following four or five principles does not befit a warlike prince.

54. When a warlike prince attacks a powerful state, his generalship shows itself in preventing the concentration of the enemy's forces. He overawes his opponents, and their allies are prevented from joining against him.

55. Hence he does not strive to ally himself with all and sundry, nor does he foster the power of other states. He carries out his own secret designs, keeping his antagonists in awe. Thus he is able to capture their cities and overthrow their kingdoms.

56. Bestow rewards without regard to rule, issue orders without regard to previous arrangements; and you will be able to handle a whole army as though you had to do with but a single man.

57. Confront your soldiers with the deed itself; never let them know your design. When the outlook is bright, bring it before their eyes; but tell them nothing when the situation is gloomy.

58. Place your army in deadly peril, and it will survive; plunge it into desperate straits, and it will come off in safety.

59. For it is precisely when a force has fallen into harm's way that it is capable of striking a blow for victory.

60. Success in warfare is gained by carefully accommodating ourselves to the enemy's purpose.

61. By persistently hanging on the enemy's flank, we shall succeed in the long run in killing the commander-in-chief.

62. This is called ability to accomplish a thing by sheer cunning.

63. On the day that you take up your command, block the frontier passes, destroy the official tallies, and stop the passage of all emissaries.

64. Be stern in the council-chamber, so that you may control the situation.

65. If the enemy leaves a door open, you must rush in.

66. Forestall your opponent by seizing what he holds dear, and subtly contrive to time his arrival on the ground.

67. Walk in the path defined by rule, and accommodate yourself to the enemy until you can fight a decisive battle.

68. At first, then, exhibit the coyness of a maiden, until the enemy gives you an opening; afterwards emulate the rapidity of a running hare, and it will be too late for the enemy to oppose you.

XII.

THE ATTACK BY FIRE

1. Sun Tzu said: There are five ways of attacking with fire. The first is to burn soldiers in their camp; the second is to burn stores; the third is to burn baggage-trains; the fourth is to burn arsenals and magazines; the fifth is to hurl dropping fire amongst the enemy.

2. In order to carry out an attack with fire, we must have means available. The material for raising fire should always be kept in readiness.

3. There is a proper season for making attacks with fire, and special days for starting a conflagration.

4. The proper season is when the weather is very dry; the special days are those when the moon is in the constellation of the Sieve, the Wall, the Wing or the Cross-bar; for these four are all days of rising wind.

5. In attacking with fire, one should be prepared to meet five possible developments:

6. (1) When fire breaks out inside the enemy's camp, respond at once with an attack from without.

7. (2) If there is an outbreak of fire, but the enemy's soldiers remain quiet, bide your time and do not attack.

8. (3) When the force of the flames has reached its height, follow it up with an attack, if that is practicable; if not, stay where you are.

9. (4) If it is possible to make an assault with fire from without, do not wait for it to break out within, but deliver your attack at a favourable moment.

10. (5) When you start a fire, be to windward of it. Do not attack from the leeward.

11. A wind that rises in the daytime lasts long, but a night breeze soon falls.

12. In every army, the five developments connected with fire must be known, the movements of the stars calculated, and a watch kept for the proper days.

13. Hence those who use fire as an aid to the attack show intelligence; those who use water as an aid to the attack gain an accession of strength.

14. By means of water, an enemy may be intercepted, but not robbed of all his belongings.

15. Unhappy is the fate of one who tries to win his battles and succeed in his attacks without cultivating the spirit of enterprise; for the result is waste of time and general stagnation.

16. Hence the saying: The enlightened ruler lays his plans well ahead; the good general cultivates his resources.

17. Move not unless you see an advantage; use not your troops unless there is something to be gained; fight not unless the position is critical.

18. No ruler should put troops into the field merely to gratify his own spleen; no general should fight a battle simply out of pique.

19. If it is to your advantage, make a forward move; if not, stay where you are.

20. Anger may in time change to gladness; vexation may be succeeded by content.

21. But a kingdom that has once been destroyed can never come again into being; nor can the dead ever be brought back to life.

22. Hence the enlightened ruler is heedful, and the good general full of caution. This is the way to keep a country at peace and an army intact.

用 間 篇

XIII.

THE USE OF SPIES

———⟋⟍———

1. Sun Tzu said: Raising a host of a hundred thousand men and marching them great distances entails heavy loss on the people and a drain on the resources of the State. The daily expenditure will amount to a thousand ounces of silver. There will be commotion at home and abroad, and men will drop down exhausted on the highways. As many as seven hundred thousand families will be impeded in their labour.

2. Hostile armies may face each other for years, striving for the victory which is decided in a single day. This being so, to remain in ignorance of the enemy's condition simply because one grudges the outlay of a hundred ounces of silver in honours and emoluments is the height of inhumanity.

3. One who acts thus is no leader of men, no present help to his sovereign, no master of victory.

4. Thus, what enables the wise sovereign and the good general to strike and conquer, and achieve things beyond the reach of ordinary men, is *foreknowledge*.

5. Now this foreknowledge cannot be elicited from spirits; it cannot be obtained inductively from experience, nor by any deductive calculation.

6. Knowledge of the enemy's dispositions can only be obtained from other men.

7. Hence the use of spies, of whom there are five classes: (1) Local spies; (2) inward spies; (3) converted spies; (4) doomed spies; (5) surviving spies.

8. When these five kinds of spy are all at work, none can discover the secret system. This is called "divine manipulation of the threads." It is the sovereign's most precious faculty.

9. Having *local spies* means employing the services of the inhabitants of a district.

10. Having *inward spies*, making use of officials of the enemy.

11. Having *converted spies*, getting hold of the enemy's spies and using them for our own purposes.

12. Having *doomed spies*, doing certain things openly for purposes of deception, and allowing our own spies to know of them and report them to the enemy.

13. *Surviving spies*, finally, are those who bring back news from the enemy's camp.

14. Hence it is that with none in the whole army are more intimate relations to be maintained than with spies. None should be more liberally rewarded. In no other business should greater secrecy be preserved.

15. Spies cannot be usefully employed without a certain intuitive sagacity.

16. They cannot be properly managed without benevolence and straightforwardness.

17. Without subtle ingenuity of mind, one cannot make certain of the truth of their reports.

18. Be subtle! Be subtle! and use your spies for every kind of business.

19. If a secret piece of news is divulged by a spy before the time is ripe, he must be put to death together with the man to whom the secret was told.

20. Whether the object be to crush an army, to storm a city, or to assassinate an individual, it is always necessary to begin by finding out the names of the attendants, the aides-de-camp, the door-keepers and sentries of the general in command. Our spies must be commissioned to ascertain these.

21. The enemy's spies who have come to spy on us must be sought out, tempted with bribes, led away and comfortably housed. Thus they will become converted spies and available for our service.

22. It is through the information brought by the converted spy that we are able to acquire and employ local and inward spies.

23. It is owing to his information, again, that we can cause the doomed spy to carry false tidings to the enemy.

24. Lastly, it is by his information that the surviving spy can be used on appointed occasions.

25. The end and aim of spying in all its five varieties is knowledge of the enemy; and this knowledge can only be derived, in the first instance, from the converted spy. Hence it is essential that the converted spy be treated with the utmost liberality.

26. Of old, the rise of the Yin dynasty was due to I Chih, who had served under the Hsia. Likewise, the rise of the Chou dynasty was due to Lü Ya, who had served under the Yin.

27. Hence it is only the enlightened ruler and the wise general who will use the highest intelligence of the army for purposes of spying, and thereby they achieve great results. Spies are a most important element in war, because on them depends an army's ability to move.

THE
ART OF WAR

with Notes, Commentaries from the
Chinese Masters, and an Appendix by
Lionel Giles and Dallas Galvin

CONTENTS

On the Translation, Notes, and Commentaries

by Dallas Galvin

Lionel Giles wanted to allow his readers to understand the text of *The Art of War* as Sun Tzu intended it. To achieve his ambition would require three tasks: creating a text able to stand alone as a work in English; indicating where the original text was uncertain; and providing English readers with some measure of the commentary—the history lessons, the strategic debates, the thoughtful qualifications—that the typical Chinese student would receive. Thus along with his translation of *The Art of War*, Giles provided copious critical notes. We have reproduced them, with emendations, along with the text as Giles originally conceived it. In addition, Giles presented commentary from some of the most important thinkers on military and historical matters throughout Chinese history.

Giles understood he was blazing a trail. At the time of the French Revolution, China had been the world's largest empire. In 1910 England held the title and was feeling the responsibility. This was the moment of high British Empire—a decade after the Boxer Rebellion, fifty years after the Indian Mutiny, and eight since the bitterly fought Boer War—when imperial reach was consolidating in Asia and Africa. Nevertheless, as an English speaker Giles was flying solo. Ever since the Enlightenment, the French and the Jesuits had made strides in translating Chinese arts and letters for the West. The Germans, the Russians, and particularly the Japanese had begun to study and translate the great Chinese classics. In this realm, however, the English were just gearing up for what would become a golden century of Asian language scholarship.

In 1905 Captain E. F. Calthrop, R.F.A., had published an English translation of *The Art of War* in Tokyo, under the Japanese name for Sun Tzu: Sonshi. Assisted by two Japanese military men, he had worked from a Japanese version of the text.

Giles dismissed Calthrop's work as substandard and not scholarly, and other scholars have rejected it too. At the turn of the
nineteenth century, Calthrop's work did not face quite the
scholarly depredation that it would by the 1930s, but it was
clearly unacceptable.

Giles's effort in 1910 was the first translation into English
of Sun Tzu's *The Art of War* by a serious sinologist. With a text
some 2,400 years old, Giles confronted a language and a sensibility at considerable remove from his own, and he worked
years before the great "Orientalists"—Arthur Waley, Ivan
Morris, Donald Keene, Burton Watson, James Legge, John
Fairbank, Owen Lattimore, and scores of poet-translators—
would fairly invent Asian studies for English speakers. Yet Giles
achieved his mission. His version can and does stand alone. It
is still studied by military men and is beloved by general readers
who have no connection to combat.

For more than fifty years, the Giles translation was the de-
finitive edition—it had no competitors. But at the opening of
the twentieth century his feat was neither easy nor assured. A
quick scan of the original Chinese text frames the issues: The
writing is neat and brief—like a haiku poem. And in several
instances, it makes no earthly sense in English or Chinese. We
need not investigate too deeply to discover why. When we encounter works like *The Art of War* we are on the long cusp of
an oral tradition. As Arthur Waley writes, "The earliest use of
connected writing . . . was as an aid to memory . . . [I]ts purpose
was to help people not to forget what they knew already,
whereas, in more advanced communities, the chief use of writing is to tell people things they have not heard before" (introduction to *The Book of Songs*, p. 11).

A completely accurate translation is categorically impossible,
always a hopeful approximation. But translators working in European tongues rarely confront the Pandora's box Giles did.
He succeeds, but not without infelicities and compromises.
Guiding his readers into this fabulous, ancient world, he introduces English words to descant the laconic Chinese text—spar-
ingly, but he does. Later translators will argue against this
practice, but they will have access to a version of the text that
is "purer" by a thousand years. And other translators will reflect
the reigning literary and cultural trends of their times. That is

the "way" of translation—Dryden and Pope, even Fitzgerald set the standard for their periods, but now they sound, if not quaint, more like themselves than a true rendering of other men's words. Language is a living thing, and as change is essential to life, it is characteristic of our words. We read Dryden's translations of Homer, Ovid, or Virgil for the devilish brilliance of Dryden's own lyricism, and even his vocabulary seems odd now, a thing apart. In *The Art of War* Giles found some measure of himself—citizen, thinker, pioneer, and, most especially, educator. That's probably why this work still stands.

Lionel Giles had to carve a passageway between West and East, Classical and contemporary, yet still keep to the text Sun Tzu composed. In the notes, Giles nails cultural and historical observations, plus the interpretations of the commentators, to the relevant phrases he translates. It is often delightful reading, but cumbersome. He wonders aloud about his choices and argues with the interpretations of other scholars, while offering wise observations about the world and its bellicose propensities. The notes break the rhythms of the original, herding the text as a sheepdog might into fields of military history, corrals of interpretive queries.

The notes are of uneven length, naturally, and do not accompany every item. We have maintained the style of the original notes but have edited them for relevance; for example, they include descriptions of Giles's methods and rationales for the translation, but such academic discussion is of interest only to linguistic scholars, and we have eliminated it here. When, for this edition, we have selected only part of a note, we have not used ellipses to show that, in the original, text precedes or follows the selection, but we have used ellipses to show omitted words within the selection.

Mere words can bridge only part of the epochal cultural chasm that exists between Sun Tzu's time and subsequent eras, even for the Chinese. Giles also faced textual interpolations and corruptions that had accreted like barnacles to the original over the millennia. For centuries, the best scholars in China had chewed over certain ideograms, argued over entire lines (or their absence), and fought over the veracity of variants of the original, just as Western scholars debate the authorship of Homer's *Iliad* and *Odyssey* and the provenance of Shakespeare's plays. Over the centuries, a great scholarly literature developed to explicate the thorny passages, to wonder over the ideograms, and to ferret out bogus additions.

Giles provides us with the most pungent and trenchant of them here in selections from the commentaries. What a gift! The authors include Wang Hsi, Ts'ao Ts'ao, Tu Yu and his grandson Tu Mu, Li Ch'üan, Mêng Shih—some of the most illustrious names in Chinese military and historical literature. They elucidate the numbered points Sun Tzu makes with examples from China's 3,000-year history, in a method that is a classic Chinese teaching device and characteristic of Chinese expository style. Apart from the delicious entrée they give us to Chinese culture, the commentaries present a print approximation for the modern reader of how an instructive treatise might have been transmitted at the time of Sun Tzu. As part of his original introduction Giles included descriptions of the major Chinese commentators he cites in the notes; they appear in this edition in the Appendix.

In this edition, we have introduced relevant excerpts from the work of Western writers and thinkers, ancient and modern—generals, poets, political leaders, and other observers.

Sun Tzu on
The Art of War

I.

LAYING PLANS

[When the enemy launched a surprise attack on Caesar's supply train] Caesar had everything to do at one time: to raise the standard . . . ; to sound the trumpet; to recall the soldiers from the fortifications; to summon those who had proceeded some distance to seek materials for a rampart; to form a battle line; to encourage the men; and to give the signal. A great part of these arrangements was prevented by the shortness of time and the sudden approach and charge of the enemy. Under these difficulties, two things proved of advantage: the soldiers' skill and experience . . . and the fact that Caesar had forbidden his several lieutenants to depart from their respective legions before the camp was fortified.

Julius Caesar, *De Bello Gallico* (58–51 B.C.)

✦ ✦ ✦

Sun Tzu signals the importance he assigns to planning by opening *The Art of War* with its discussion—and then reiterating many of the points from this chapter through subsequent chapters. While we cannot know with certainty whether the Greeks and the Romans studied Sun Tzu's work, they must have known it at least indirectly. Across the centuries caravansaries plied the Silk Road, exchanging cultural tidbits far less valuable between China and empires to the West.   DG

---

    1. Sun Tzu said: The art of war is of vital importance to the State.

    2. It is a matter of life and death, a road either to safety or

to ruin. Hence it is a subject of inquiry which can on no account be neglected.

3. The art of war, then, is governed by five constant factors, to be taken into account in one's deliberations, when seeking to determine the conditions obtaining in the field.

4. These are: (1) The Moral Law; (2) Heaven; (3) Earth; (4) The Commander; (5) Method and discipline.

It appears from what follows that Sun Tzu means by Moral Law a principle of harmony, not unlike the Tao [method or way] of Lao Tzu in its moral aspect. One might be tempted to render it by "morale," were it not considered as an attribute of the *ruler* in paragraph 13.

We have here the fundamental problem of ethics, the crux of the theory of moral conduct. What is justice?—shall we seek righteousness, or shall we seek power?—is it better to be good, or to be strong?

Will Durant, *The Story of Philosophy* (1926)

5, 6. *The Moral Law* causes the people to be in complete accord with their ruler, so that they will follow him regardless of their lives, undismayed by any danger.

If, for example, good meant intelligent, and virtue meant wisdom; if men could be taught to see clearly their real interests, to see afar the distant results of their deeds, to criticize and coördinate their desires out of a self-canceling chaos into a purposive and creative harmony—this, perhaps, would provide for the educated and sophisticated man the morality which in the unlettered relies on re-iterated precepts and external control.

Will Durant, *The Story of Philosophy* (1926)

---

7. *Heaven* signifies night and day, cold and heat, times and seasons.

Wang Hsi [see "Appendix: The Commentators"] . . . may be right in saying that what is meant is "the general economy of Heaven," including the five elements, the four seasons, wind and clouds, and other phenomena.

Though from the earliest times the Chinese were monotheistic, by Sun Tzu's era various lesser deities associated with the seasons and the elements had taken hold. DG

8. *Earth* comprises distances, great and small; danger and security; open ground and narrow passes; the chances of life and death.

For Sun Tzu, *heaven* and *earth* conjure the conditions and the situations, as much as the physical terrain, whereby moral law is made manifest and played out. DG

9. *The Commander* stands for the virtues of wisdom, sincerity, benevolence, courage and strictness.

The five cardinal virtues of the Chinese are (1) humanity or benevolence; (2) uprightness of mind; (3) self-respect, self-control, or "proper feeling"; (4) wisdom; (5) sincerity or good faith. Here wisdom and sincerity are put before humanity, and the two military virtues of "courage" and "strictness" [are] substituted for uprightness and self-respect.

10. By *Method and discipline* are to be understood the marshalling of the army in its proper subdivisions, the gradations of rank among the officers, the maintenance of roads by which supplies may reach the army, and the control of military expenditure.

11. These five heads should be familiar to every general: he who knows them will be victorious; he who knows them not will fail.

12. Therefore, in your deliberations, when seeking to determine the military conditions, let them be made the basis of a comparison, in this wise:

13. (1) Which of the two sovereigns is imbued with the Moral Law?

I.e., "is in harmony with his subjects."

(2) Which of the two generals has most ability?
(3) With whom lie the advantages derived from Heaven and Earth?
(4) On which side is discipline most rigorously enforced?

Tu Mu alludes to the remarkable story of Ts'ao Ts'ao (A.D.155–220), who was such a strict disciplinarian that once, in accordance with his own severe regulations against injury to standing crops, he condemned himself to death for having allowed his horse to shy into a field of corn! However, in lieu of losing his head, he was persuaded to satisfy his sense of justice by cutting off his hair. Ts'ao Ts'ao's own comment on the present passage is characteristically curt: "When you lay down a law, see that it is not disobeyed; if it is disobeyed, the offender must be put to death."

(5) Which army is the stronger?

Morally as well as physically.

(6) On which side are officers and men more highly trained?

Tu Yu quotes [another commentator]: "Without constant practice, the officers will be nervous and undecided when mustering for battle; without constant practice, the general will be wavering and irresolute when the crisis is at hand."

(7) In which army is there the greater constancy both in reward and punishment?

That is, on which side is there the most absolute certainty that merit will be properly rewarded and misdeeds summarily punished?

> It is certainly for the interest of the service that a cordial inter-change of civilities should subsist between superior and inferior officers, and therefore it is bad policy in superiors to behave toward their inferiors indiscriminately, as tho' they were of a lower species, such a conduct will damp the spirits of any man. . . . Cheerful ardor and spirit . . . ought ever to be the characteristic of an officer . . . for to be well obeyed it is necessary to be esteemed.
>
>   John Paul Jones (1776)

14. By means of these seven considerations I can forecast victory or defeat.

Who does what, and how the activities are organized (in counterguerrilla or guerrilla warfare), is far less important than understanding the mission and being determined to accomplish it by means not inconsistent with the mission. So long as a sufficient number understand the mission and what it implies, seek to accomplish it with a dedication and an intelligence not substantially inferior to that of the enemy, and receive adequate political support, the counterguerrilla effort should not usually be difficult.

Lt. Col. Charles Bohannan and Col. Napoleon Valeriano,
Counterguerrilla Operations (1962)

15. The general that hearkens to my counsel and acts upon it, will conquer:—let such a one be retained in command! The general that hearkens not to my counsel nor acts upon it, will suffer defeat:—let such a one be dismissed!

The form of this paragraph reminds us that Sun Tzu's treatise was composed expressly for the benefit of his patron, Ho Lü, king of the Wu State.

16. While heeding the profit of my counsel, avail yourself also of any helpful circumstances over and beyond the ordinary rules.

17. According as circumstances are favourable, one should modify one's plans.

Sun Tzu, as a practical soldier, will have none of the "bookish theoric." He cautions us here not to pin our faith to abstract principles; "for," as Chang Yü puts it, "while the main laws of strategy can be stated clearly enough for the benefit of all and sundry, you must be guided by the actions of the enemy in attempting to secure a favourable position in actual warfare." On the eve of the battle of Waterloo, Lord Uxbridge, commanding the cavalry, went to the Duke of Wellington in order to learn what his plans and calculations were for the morrow, because, as he explained, he might suddenly find himself Commander-in-chief and would be unable to frame new plans in a critical moment. The Duke listened quietly and then said, "Who will attack first to-morrow—I or Bonaparte?" "Bonaparte," replied Lord Uxbridge. "Well," continued the

Duke, "Bonaparte has not given me any idea of his projects; and as my plans will depend upon his, how can you expect me to tell you what mine are?"

_____

18. All warfare is based on deception.

The truth of this pithy and profound saying will be admitted by every soldier. Col. Henderson [Lt. Col. G. F. R. Henderson, author of *Stonewall Jackson and the American Civil War* (1898) and *The Science of War* (1905)] tells us that Wellington, great in so many military qualities, was especially distinguished by the "extraordinary skill with which he concealed his movements and deceived both friend and foe."

_____

This is *the* great, famous line from *The Art of War*, quoted through the ages.   DG

_____

19. Hence, when able to attack, we must seem unable; when using our forces, we must seem inactive; when we are near, we must make the enemy believe we are far away; when far away, we must make him believe we are near.

20. Hold out baits to entice the enemy. Feign disorder, and crush him.

21. If he is secure at all points, be prepared for him. If he is in superior strength, evade him.

22. If your opponent is of choleric temper, seek to irritate him. Pretend to be weak, that he may grow arrogant.

Wang Tzu, quoted by Tu Yu, says that the good tactician plays with his adversary as a cat plays with a mouse, first feigning weakness and immobility, and then suddenly pouncing upon him.

_____

23. If he is taking his ease, give him no rest.

24. Attack him where he is unprepared, appear where you are not expected.

To what Federal soldier did it occur, on the morning of Chancellorsville, that [General Robert E.] Lee, confronted by 90,000 Northerners, would detach the half of his own small force of 50,000 to attack his enemy in flank and rear? ... [The Battle of Chancellorsville] took place in May 1863. Lee's maneuvers, in conjunction with General Thomas "Stonewall" Jackson's devastating surprise attack, are still studied in military academies.

George Francis Robert Henderson and Sir Thomas Barclay, "War," *Encyclopedia Britannica*, eleventh edition (1910)

25. These military devices, leading to victory, must not be divulged beforehand.

This . . . is perhaps the best sense to be got out of the text as it stands. Most of the commentators give the following explanation: "It is impossible to lay down rules for warfare before you come into touch with the enemy."

26. Now the general who wins a battle makes many calculations in his temple ere the battle is fought.

Chang Yü tells us that in ancient times it was customary for a temple to be set apart for the use of a general who was about to take the field, in order that he might there elaborate his plan of campaign.

The general who loses a battle makes but few calculations beforehand. Thus do many calculations lead to victory, and few calculations to defeat: how much more no calculation at all! It is by attention to this point that I can foresee who is likely to win or lose.

作 戰 篇

II.

WAGING WAR

———— ✒ ————

Coin is the sinews of war.
> François Rabelais, *Gargantua and Pantagruel* (1532)

An army marches on its stomach.
> Napoleon I, quoted in *Mémorial de Ste-Hélène*, by Emmanuel, comte de Las Cases (1823)

◆ ◆ ◆

The main themes of this chapter—the costs of war, the speed with which it is waged, the need to secure good lines of supply, and the requirement of fast movement (fluidity)—are essential to battle, be it guerrilla or traditional warfare. Particularly in the case of fluidity and its concomitant, negative space, these concepts were at one time considered quintessentially "Asian" by military historians.

European culture, contrariwise, they would claim, put its stock in masses, blocks, and bulk. Broadly conceived, think of skyscrapers and epic poetry versus pagodas and haiku, boxing versus tai chi, the huge destroyers of World War II versus kamikazes. Apples and oranges, of course, but that's the point. The images pose for us a singular difference in cultural emphasis and era. Influential anthropologist Franz Boas insisted that "great" cultures could be divined by the size of their cities and monuments, their accumulation of goods. In the media-dense, peripatetic world of today, where multinational peacekeeping forces exchange notes across borders, those differences are melting away, but in American wars as recent as Korea and Vietnam, the differences literally gave rise to success or loss in battle after battle.

The first translation of *The Art of War* into a Western language was by a French Jesuit, Jean-Joseph M. Amiot, in the late 1700s, and it caused a great stir. We can be reasonably sure that Napoleon I was aware of the military and scientific ideas of the Chinese. He would have seen the work as confirming his own strategic credo of *fluidity*: not being where the enemy expects you, appearing always where he least expects, and extraordinary speed in battle. Napoleon insisted in his *Maxims*: "One must be slow in deliberation and quick in execution."   DG

Ts'ao Kung has the note, "He who wishes to fight must first count the cost," which prepares us for the discovery that the subject of the chapter is not what we might expect from the title, but is primarily a consideration of ways and means.

---

1. Sun Tzu said: In the operations of war, where there are in the field a thousand swift chariots, as many heavy chariots, and a hundred thousand mail-clad soldiers,

---

The swift chariots were lightly built and, according to Chang Yü, used for the attack; the heavy chariots were . . . designed for purposes of defence. . . . It is interesting to note the analogies between early Chinese warfare and that of the Homeric Greeks. In each case, the war-chariot was the important factor, forming as it did the nucleus round which was grouped a certain number of foot-soldiers. . . . We are informed that each swift chariot was accompanied by 75 footmen or infantry, and each heavy chariot by 25 footmen, so that the whole army would be divided up into a thousand battalions, each consisting of two chariots and a hundred men.

---

with provisions enough to carry them a thousand *li*,

2.78 modern *li* go to a mile. The length may have varied slightly since Sun Tzu's time.

---

the expenditure at home and at the front, including entertainment of guests, small items such as glue and paint, and sums spent on chariots and armour, will reach the total of a thousand ounces of silver per day. Such is the cost of raising an army of 100,000 men.

2. When you engage in actual fighting, if victory is long in

coming, the men's weapons will grow dull and their ardour will
be damped. If you lay siege to a town, you will exhaust your
strength.

> The greatest good deed in war is the speedy ending of the war,
> and every means to that end, so long as it is not reprehensible,
> must remain open.
>
> Count Helmuth von Moltke, "On the Nature of War" (1880)

3. Again, if the campaign is protracted, the resources of the
State will not be equal to the strain.

> Commerce diminishes the spirit, both of patriotism and military
> defense. And history sufficiently informs us, that the bravest
> achievements were always accomplished in the non-age of a na-
> tion. . . . The more men have to lose, the less willing are they to
> venture. The rich are in general slaves to fear, and submit to
> courtly power with the trembling duplicity of a spaniel.
>
> Thomas Paine, *Common Sense* (1776)

4. Now, when your weapons are dulled, your ardour
damped, your strength exhausted and your treasure spent, other
chieftains will spring up to take advantage of your extremity.
Then no man, however wise, will be able to avert the consequences that must ensue.

5. Thus, though we have heard of stupid haste in war, cleverness has never been seen associated with long delays.

This concise and difficult sentence is not well explained by any of the
commentators. [Six commentators suggest] that a general, though naturally stupid, may nevertheless conquer through sheer force of rapidity.
Ho Shih says: "Haste may be stupid, but at any rate it saves expenditure
of energy and treasure; protracted operations may be very clever, but
they bring calamity in their train." Wang Hsi evades the difficulty by
remarking: "Lengthy operations mean an army growing old, wealth being expended, an empty exchequer and distress among the people; true
cleverness insures against the occurrence of such calamities." Chang Yü
says: "So long as victory can be attained, stupid haste is preferable to
clever dilatoriness."

Now Sun Tzu says nothing whatever, except possibly by implication, about ill-considered haste being better than ingenious but lengthy operations. What he does say is something much more guarded, namely that, while speed may sometimes be injudicious, tardiness can never be anything but foolish—if only because it means impoverishment to the nation. . . .

In considering the point raised here by Sun Tzu, the classic example of Fabius Cunctator will inevitably occur to the mind. That general deliberately measured the endurance of Rome against that of Hannibal's isolated army, because it seemed to him that the latter was more likely to suffer from a long campaign in a strange country. But it is quite a moot question whether his tactics would have proved successful in the long run. Their reversal, it is true, led to Cannae [a huge defeat for the Romans under his successor]; but this only establishes a negative presumption in their favour.

Fabius Maximus Cunctator, Quintus, Roman statesman and military commander, was known as "the Delayer." His use of long delays in the Second Punic War wore down the resistance of Hannibal's Carthaginian army and decimated their supply lines, giving Rome a savage victory.   DG

---

6. There is no instance of a country having benefited from prolonged warfare.

We hear war called murder. It is not: it is suicide.
British Prime Minister James Ramsay MacDonald (1930)

---

7. It is only one who is thoroughly acquainted with the evils of war that can thoroughly understand the profitable way of carrying it on.

That is, with rapidity. Only one who knows the disastrous effects of a long war can realise the supreme importance of rapidity in bringing it to a close.

---

8. The skilful soldier does not raise a second levy, neither are his supply-wagons loaded more than twice.

Once war is declared, he will not waste precious time in waiting for reinforcements, nor will he turn his army back for fresh supplies, but crosses the enemy's frontier without delay. This may seem an audacious policy to recommend, but with all great strategists, from Julius Caesar to Napoleon Buonaparte, the value of time—that is, being a little ahead of your opponent—has counted for more than either numerical superiority or the nicest calculations with regard to commissariat [food supplies].

I don't want to get any messages saying, "I am holding my position." We are not holding a goddamned thing. Let the Germans do that. We are advancing constantly, and we are not interested in holding onto anything except the enemies' balls. . . . Our basic plan of operation is to advance and to keep on advancing regardless of whether we have to go over, under, or through the enemy. We are going to go through him like crap through a goose.

Gen. George S. Patton, speech to the Third Army on the eve of the Allied invasion of France (1944)

---

9. Bring war material with you from home, but forage on the enemy. Thus the army will have food enough for its needs.

10. Poverty of the State exchequer causes an army to be maintained by contributions from a distance. Contributing to maintain an army at a distance causes the people to be impoverished.

11. On the other hand, the proximity of an army causes prices to go up, and high prices cause the people's substance to be drained away.

12. When their substance is drained away, the peasantry will be afflicted by heavy exactions.

13, 14. With this loss of substance and exhaustion of strength, the homes of the people will be stripped bare, and three-tenths of their incomes will be dissipated; while Government expenses for broken chariots, worn-out horses, breast-plates and helmets, bows and arrows, spears and shields, protective mantlets, draught-oxen and heavy waggons, will amount to four-tenths of its total revenue.

15. Hence a wise general makes a point of foraging on the enemy. One carload of the enemy's provisions is equivalent to twenty of one's own, and likewise a single *picul* of his provender is equivalent to twenty from one's own store.

Because twenty carloads will be consumed in the process of transporting one cartload to the front.

---

16. Now in order to kill the enemy, our men must be roused to anger; that there may be advantage from defeating the enemy, they must have their rewards.

Tu Mu says: "Rewards are necessary in order to make the soldiers see the advantage of beating the enemy; thus, when you capture spoils from the enemy, they must be used as rewards, so that all your men may have a keen desire to fight, each on his own account."

---

17. Therefore in chariot fighting, when ten or more chariots have been taken, those should be rewarded who took the first. Our own flags should be substituted for those of the enemy, and the chariots mingled and used in conjunction with ours. The captured soldiers should be kindly treated and kept.

18. This is called, using the conquered foe to augment one's own strength.

19. In war, then, let your great object be victory, not lengthy campaigns.

Yours is the profession of arms, the will to win, the sure knowledge that in war, there is no substitute for victory.
   Gen. Douglas MacArthur, speech at West Point (1962)

---

20. Thus it may be known that the leader of armies is the arbiter of the people's fate, the man on whom it depends whether the nation shall be in peace or in peril.

In Chinese historiography it is still the will of the individual which directs the course of history.
   Burton Watson, *Early Chinese Literature* (1962)

I came, I saw, I conquered.
   Julius Caesar, quoted in *Plutarch's Lives* (A.D. 75)

謀攻篇

III.

ATTACK BY STRATAGEM

⟶⟨⟩⟶

The general himself ought to be such a one as can at the same
time see both forward and backward.

Plutarch, *Moralia* (A.D. 75)

◆ ◆ ◆

1. Sun Tzu said: In the practical art of war, the best thing
of all is to take the enemy's country whole and intact; to shatter
and destroy it is not so good. So, too, it is better to capture an
army entire than to destroy it, to capture a regiment, a detachment or a company entire than to destroy them.

The Denma Translation is worth comparing here (see "For Further
Reading"). Closer to the astringent sound and pared rhythms of
the Classical Chinese text, it reads: "In sum, the method of employing the military—Taking a state whole is superior. Destroying it is
inferior to this. Taking an army whole is superior. Destroying it is inferior to this. Taking a battalion whole is superior. Destroying it is inferior
to this. Taking a company whole is superior. Destroying it is inferior to
this. Taking a squad whole is superior. Destroying it is inferior
to this."   DG

2. Hence to fight and conquer in all your battles is not supreme excellence; supreme excellence consists in breaking the
enemy's resistance without fighting.

Here again, no modern strategist but will approve the words of [Sun Tzu]. Moltke's greatest triumph, the capitulation of the huge French army at Sedan, was won practically without bloodshed.

———————

3. Thus the highest form of generalship is to baulk the enemy's plans;

I.e., as Li Ch'üan says, in their very inception. Perhaps the word "baulk" falls short of expressing the full force of [the Chinese term], which implies not an attitude of defence, whereby one might be content to foil the enemy's stratagems one after another, but an active policy of counter-attack. Ho Shih put this very clearly in his note: "When the enemy has made a plan of attack against us, we must anticipate him by delivering our own attack first."

———————

the next best is to prevent the junction of the enemy's forces;

Isolating him from his allies. We must not forget that Sun Tzu, in speaking of hostilities, always has in mind the numerous states or principalities into which the China of his day was split up.

———————

the next in order is to attack the enemy's army in the field;

When he is already in full strength.

———————

and the worst policy of all is to besiege walled cities.

4. The rule is, not to besiege walled cities if it can possibly be avoided.

Another sound piece of military theory. Had the Boers acted upon it in 1899, and refrained from dissipating their strength before Kimberley, Mafeking, or even Ladysmith, it is more than probable that they would have been masters of the situation before the British were ready seriously to oppose them.

———————

Kimberley, Mafeking, and Ladysmith were all important early defeats for the British against the Boer insurgency. The British regulars badly underestimated their colonial foes in what was essentially a war for independence: the South African War. The details of the siege, the battles, and the final British response are worth examining in greater detail both to capture Giles's full meaning here and also because they read like a petri dish exemplar of Sun Tzu's admonitions on tactics. Turn to the early writings of Winston Churchill for a pithy examination of the war from the perspective of a participant whose life was deeply affected by it.

The gist of Giles's comment, however, is that the Boers (Dutch South Africans) initially had the jump on the British. They dissipated their military energies, however, in "small," brutal engagements, such as the siege at Ladysmith, which they besieged from October 1899 through February 1900, causing the deaths of several thousand citizens. This gave the British time to dispatch formidable regiments from England. Because of its strategic geography, South Africa was important to the British Empire both for its considerable natural resources and also as a protection for their colonial properties, especially India. Ladysmith, for example, is in the Natal region, which had long served as a gateway to the Indian Ocean.   DG

The preparation of mantlets, movable shelters, and various implements of war, will take up three whole months;

It is not quite clear what mantlets were. Ts'ao Kung simply defines them as "large shields," but we get a better idea of them from Li Ch'üan, who says they were to protect the heads of those who were assaulting the city walls at close quarters. This seems to suggest a sort of Roman *testudo*, ready made. Tu Mu says they were . . . (wheeled vehicles used in repelling attacks, according to K'ang Hsi). . . . The name is also applied to turrets on city walls.

Of movable shelters, we get a fairly clear description from several commentators. They were wooden missile-proof structures on four wheels, propelled from within, covered over with raw hides, and used in sieges to convey parties of men to and from the walls, for the purpose of filling up the encircling moat with earth. Tu Mu adds that they are now called "wooden donkeys."

---

and the piling up of mounds over against the walls will take three months more.

These were great mounds or ramparts of earth heaped up to the level of the enemy's walls in order to discover the weak points in the defence, and also to destroy the fortified turrets mentioned in the preceding note.

---

5. The general, unable to control his irritation, will launch his men to the assault like swarming ants,

This vivid simile . . . is taken from the spectacle of an army of ants climbing a wall. The meaning is that the general, losing patience at the long delay, may make a premature attempt to storm the place before his engines of war are ready.

———————

with the result that one-third of his men are slain, while the town still remains untaken. Such are the disastrous effects of a siege.

6. Therefore the skilful leader subdues the enemy's troops without any fighting; he captures their cities without laying siege to them; he overthrows their kingdom without lengthy operations in the field.

Chia Lin notes that he only overthrows the . . . Government, but does no harm to individuals. The classical instance is Wu Wang, who after having put an end to the Yin dynasty was acclaimed "Father and mother of the people."

———————

7. With his forces intact he will dispute the mastery of the Empire, and thus, without losing a man, his triumph will be complete.

Owing to . . . double meanings . . . , the latter part of the sentence is susceptible of quite a different meaning: "And thus, the weapon, not being blunted by use, its keenness remains perfect."

———————

> The 101ˢᵗ has no history, but it has a rendezvous with destiny.
>> Maj. Gen. William C. Lee, rallying the men of the nascent 101ˢᵗ Airborne Division (1942)

———————

This is the method of attacking by stratagem.

8. It is the rule in war, if our forces are ten to the enemy's one, to surround him; if five to one, to attack him;

Straightaway, without waiting for any further advantage.

———————

if twice as numerous, to divide our army into two.

The saying . . . at first sight . . . appears to violate a fundamental principle of war. Ts'ao Kung, however, gives a clue to Sun Tzu's meaning: "Being two to the enemy's one, we may use one part of our army in the regular way, and the other for some special diversion." Chang Yü thus further elucidates the point: "If our force is twice as numerous as that of the enemy, it should be split up into two divisions, one to meet the enemy in front, and one to fall upon his rear; if he replies to the frontal attack, he may be crushed from behind; if to the rearward attack, he may be crushed in front."

9. If equally matched, we can offer battle;

Li Ch'üan, followed by Ho Shih, gives the following paraphrase: "If attackers and attacked are equally matched in strength, only the able general will fight."

> When the enemy is equal in the number of its forces, there should be an immediate retreat, and then the enemy should be ambushed or eliminated by means of sharp-shooters.
> U.S. Dept. of the Army, *Handbook on Aggressor Insurgent Warfare* (1962 edition)

if slightly inferior in numbers, we can avoid the enemy;

Chang Yü reminds us that the saying only applies if the other factors are equal; a small difference in numbers is often more than counterbalanced by superior energy and discipline.

if quite unequal in every way, we can flee from him.

10. Hence, though an obstinate fight may be made by a small force, in the end it must be captured by the larger force.

11. Now the general is the bulwark of the State: if the bulwark is complete at all points, the State will be strong; if the bulwark is defective, the State will be weak.

As Li Ch'üan tersely puts it: ". . . If the general's ability is not perfect (*i.e.*, if he is not thoroughly versed in his profession), his army will lack strength."

12. There are three ways in which a ruler can bring misfortune upon his army:—

13. (1) By commanding the army to advance or to retreat, being ignorant of the fact that it cannot obey. This is called hobbling the army.

"Hobbling the army" is one of those graphic metaphors which from time to time illuminate Sun Tzu's work. . . . Li Ch'üan . . . adds the comment, "It is like tying together the legs of a thoroughbred, so that it is unable to gallop." One would naturally think of "the ruler" in this passage as being at home, and trying to direct the movements of his army from a distance. But the commentators understand just the reverse, and quote the saying of T'ai Kung: "A kingdom should not be governed from without, an army should not be directed from within." Of course it is true that, during an engagement, or when in close touch with the enemy, the general should not be in the thick of his own troops, but a little distance apart. Otherwise, he will be liable to misjudge the position as a whole, and give wrong orders.

———————

14. (2) By attempting to govern an army in the same way as he administers a kingdom, being ignorant of the conditions which obtain in an army. This causes restlessness in the soldiers' minds.

Ts'ao Kung's note is . . . : "The military sphere and the civil sphere are wholly distinct; you can't handle an army in kid gloves." And Chang Yü says: "Humanity and justice are the principles on which to govern a state, but not an army; opportunism and flexibility, on the other hand, are military rather than civic virtues."

———————

15. (3) By employing the officers of his army without discrimination, through ignorance of the military principle of adaptation to circumstances. This shakes the confidence of the soldiers.

Tu Mu [quotes another commentator]: "The skilful employer of men will employ the wise man, the brave man, the covetous man, and the stupid man. For the wise man delights in establishing his merit, the brave man likes to show his courage in action, the covetous man is quick at seizing advantages, and the stupid man has no fear of death."

———————

16. But when the army is restless and distrustful, trouble is sure to come from the other feudal princes. This is simply bringing anarchy into the army, and flinging victory away.

17. Thus we may know that there are five essentials for victory:

> (1) He will win who knows when to fight and when not to fight.

Chang Yü says: "If he can fight, he advances and takes the offensive; if he cannot fight, he retreats and remains on the defensive. He will invariably conquer who knows whether it is right to take the offensive or the defensive."

_____

> (2) He will win who knows how to handle both superior and inferior forces.

This is not merely the general's ability to estimate numbers correctly. . . . Chang Yü expounds the saying more satisfactorily: "By applying the art of war, it is possible with a lesser force to defeat a greater, and *vice versa*. The secret lies in an eye for locality, and in not letting the right moment slip. Thus Wu Tzu says: 'With a superior force, make for easy ground; with an inferior one, make for difficult ground.' "

_____

After *The Art of War*, the treatise referred to as *Wu Tzu* (written by Wu Ch'i, who died in 381 B.C.) is probably the oldest military work in Chinese history and the one cited most often.   DG

_____

> (3) He will win whose army is animated by the same spirit throughout all its ranks.
> (4) He will win who, prepared himself, waits to take the enemy unprepared.
> (5) He will win who has military capacity and is not interfered with by the sovereign.

Tu Yu quotes [another commentator] as saying: "It is the sovereign's function to give broad instructions, but to decide on battle is the function of the general." It is needless to dilate on the military disasters which have been caused by undue interference with operations in the field on the part of the home government. Napoleon undoubtedly owed much of his extraordinary success to the fact that he was not hampered by any central authority.

_____

Victory lies in the knowledge of these five points.

Literally, "These five things are knowledge of the principle of victory."

———

18. Hence the saying: If you know the enemy and know yourself, you need not fear the result of a hundred battles. If you know yourself but not the enemy, for every victory gained you will also suffer a defeat.

Li Ch'üan cites the case of Fu Chien, prince of Ch'in, who in 383 A.D. marched with a vast army against the Chin Emperor. When warned not to despise an enemy who could command the services of such men as Hsieh An and Huan Ch'ung, he boastfully replied: "I have the population of eight provinces at my back, infantry and horsemen to the number of one million; why, they could dam up the Yangtsze River itself by merely throwing their whips into the stream. What danger have I to fear?" Nevertheless, his forces were soon after disastrously routed at the Fei River, and he was obliged to beat a hasty retreat.

———

If you know neither the enemy nor yourself, you will succumb in every battle.

Chang Yü offers the best commentary. . . . He says that these words "have reference to attack and defence: knowing the enemy enables you to take the offensive, knowing yourself enables you to stand on the defensive." He adds, "Attack is the secret of defence; defence is the planning of an attack." It would be hard to find a better epitome of the root-principle of war.

———

This man, I say, is most perfect who shall have understood everything for himself, after having devised what may be best afterward and unto the end.

Hesiod, *Works and Days* (c.800 B.C.)

———

形 篇

IV.

TACTICAL DISPOSITIONS

⎯⎯⎯⎯

Where force is necessary, there it must be applied boldly, decisively, and completely. But one must know the limitations of force; one must know when to blend force with a maneuver, a blow with an argument.

Leon Trotsky (1932)

✦ ✦ ✦

The Chinese given as the heading here is a very comprehensive and somewhat vague term. . . . It is best taken as something between, or perhaps combining, "tactics" and "disposition of troops." Ts'ao Kung explains it as "marching and countermarching on the part of the two armies with a view to discovering each other's condition." Tu Mu says: "It is through the dispositions of an army that its condition may be discovered. Conceal your dispositions, and your condition will remain secret, which leads to victory; show your dispositions, and your condition will become patent, which leads to defeat." Wang Hsi remarks that the good general can "secure success by modifying his tactics to meet those of the enemy."

⎯⎯⎯⎯

1. Sun Tzu said: The good fighters of old first put themselves beyond the possibility of defeat, and then waited for an opportunity of defeating the enemy.

2. To secure ourselves against defeat lies in our own hands, but the opportunity of defeating the enemy is provided by the enemy himself.

That is, of course, by a mistake on his part.

3. Thus the good fighter is able to secure himself against defeat,

Chang Yü says: "By concealing the disposition of his troops, covering up his tracks, and taking unremitting precautions."

but cannot make certain of defeating the enemy.

4. Hence the saying: One may *know* how to conquer without being able to *do* it.

5. Security against defeat implies defensive tactics; ability to defeat the enemy means taking the offensive.

The commentators are all against me. The meaning they give, "He who cannot conquer takes the defensive," is plausible enough, but . . . highly improbable.

6. Standing on the defensive indicates insufficient strength; attacking, a superabundance of strength.

7. The general who is skilled in defence hides in the most secret recesses of the earth;

Literally, "hides under the ninth earth," which is a metaphor indicating the utmost secrecy and concealment, so that the enemy may not know his whereabouts.

> Batista has 3,000 men in the field against us. It is a battle against time, and time is on our side. They never know where we are, but we always know where they are.
>
> Fidel Castro (February 24, 1957)

he who is skilled in attack flashes forth from the topmost heights of heaven.

Another metaphor, implying that he falls on his adversary like a thunderbolt, against which there is no time to prepare. This is the opinion of most of the commentators, though Ts'ao Kung, followed by Tu Yu, explains "secret recesses" as the hills, rivers, and other natural features which will afford shelter or protection to the attacked, and "topmost heights of heaven" as the phases of weather which may be turned to account by the attacking party.

———————

Thus on the one hand we have ability to protect ourselves; on the other, a victory that is complete.

8. To see victory only when it is within the ken of the common herd is not the acme of excellence.

As Ts'ao Kung remarks, "The thing is to see the plant before it has germinated," to foresee the event before the action has begun. Li Ch'üan alludes to the story of Han Hsin who, when about to attack the vastly superior army of Chao, which was strongly entrenched in the city of Ch'êng-an, said to his officers, "Gentlemen, we are going to annihilate the enemy, and shall meet again at dinner." The officers hardly took his words seriously, and gave a very dubious assent. But Han Hsin had already worked out in his mind the details of a clever stratagem, whereby, as he foresaw, he was able to capture the city and inflict a crushing defeat on his adversary.

———————

9. Neither is it the acme of excellence if you fight and conquer and the whole Empire says, "Well done!"

True excellence being, as Tu Mu says: "To plan secretly, to move surreptitiously, to foil the enemy's intentions and baulk his schemes, so that at last the day may be won without shedding a drop of blood." Sun Tzu reserves his approbation for things that

> "the world's coarse thumb
> And finger fail to plumb."

———————

10. To lift an autumn hair is no sign of great strength; to see sun and moon is no sign of sharp sight; to hear the noise of thunder is no sign of a quick ear.

11. What the ancients called a clever fighter is one who not only wins, but excels in winning with ease.

Mei Yao-ch'ên says: "He who only sees the obvious, wins his battles with difficulty; he who looks below the surface of things, wins with ease."

———————

12. Hence his victories bring him neither reputation for wisdom nor credit for courage.

Tu Mu explains this very well, "Inasmuch as his victories are gained over circumstances that have not come to light, the world at large knows nothing of them, and he wins no reputation for wisdom; inasmuch as the hostile state submits before there has been any bloodshed, he receives no credit for courage."

13. He wins his battles by making no mistakes.

Ch'ên Hao says: "He plans no superfluous marches, he devises no futile attacks." The connection of ideas is thus explained by Chang Yü: "One who seeks to conquer by sheer strength, clever though he may be at winning pitched battles, is also liable on occasion to be vanquished; whereas he who can look into the future and discern conditions that are not yet manifest, will never make a blunder and therefore invariably win."

Making no mistakes is what establishes the certainty of victory, for it means conquering an enemy that is already defeated.

14. Hence the skilful fighter puts himself into a position which makes defeat impossible, and does not miss the moment for defeating the enemy.

Position need not be confined strictly to the actual ground occupied by the troops. It includes all the arrangements and preparations which a wise general will make to increase the safety of his army.

15. Thus it is that in war the victorious strategist only seeks battle after the victory has been won, whereas he who is destined to defeat first fights and afterwards looks for victory.

Ho Shih thus expounds the paradox: "In warfare, first lay plans which will ensure victory, and then lead your army to battle; if you will not begin with stratagem but rely on brute strength alone, victory will no longer be assured."

We make this wide encircling movement in the Mediterranean, having for its primary object the recovery of the command of that vital sea, but also having for its object the exposure of the under-belly of the Axis, especially Italy, to every attack.

Winston Churchill, debate in House of Commons (1942)

16. The consummate leader cultivates the moral law, and strictly adheres to method and discipline; thus it is in his power to control success.

> There is a very strong temptation . . . for government forces to act outside the law, the excuses being that the processes of law are too cumbersome, that the normal safeguards in the law for the individual are not designed for an insurgency and that a terrorist deserves to be treated as an outlaw anyway. Not only is this morally wrong, but, over a period, it will create more practical difficulties for a government than it solves. A government which does not act in accordance with the law forfeits the right to be called a government and cannot expect its people to obey the law. Functioning in accordance with the law is a very small price to pay in return for the advantage of being the government.
> Sir Robert Grainger Ker Thompson, *Defeating Communist Insurgency: Experiences from Malaya and Vietnam* (1966)

17. In respect of military method, we have, firstly, Measurement; secondly, Estimation of quantity; thirdly, Calculation; fourthly, Balancing of chances; fifthly, Victory.

18. Measurement owes its existence to Earth; Estimation of quantity to Measurement; Calculation to Estimation of quantity; Balancing of chances to Calculation; and Victory to Balancing of chances.

It is not easy to distinguish [these] four terms very clearly. The first seems to be surveying and measurement of the ground, which enable us to form an estimate of the enemy's strength, and to make calculations based on the data thus obtained; we are thus led to a general weighing-up, or comparison of the enemy's chances with our own; if the latter turn the scale, then victory ensues.

19. A victorious army opposed to a routed one, is as a pound's weight placed in the scale against a single grain.

Literally, "a victorious army is like an *i* (20 oz.) weighed against a *shu* (1/24 oz.); a routed army as a *shu* weighted against an *i*." The point is simply the enormous advantage which a disciplined force, flushed with victory, has over one demoralised by defeat.

20. The onrush of a conquering force is like the bursting of pent-up waters into a chasm a thousand fathoms deep. So much for tactical dispositions.

V.

ENERGY

The battle swayed. / Half-naked men hacked slowly at each other
/ As the Greeks eased back the Trojans. / They stood close; /
Closer; thigh in thigh; mask twisted over iron mask / Like kissing.
  Christopher Logue, *War Music* (1987)

✦ ✦ ✦

Wang Hsi expands ["energy"] into "the application, in various ways, of
accumulated power"; and Chang Yü says: "When the soldiers' energy
has reached its height, it may be used to secure victory."

———

1. Sun Tzu said: The control of a large force is the same in
principle as the control of a few men: it is merely a question
of dividing up their numbers.

That is, cutting up the army into regiments, companies, etc., with subordinate officers in command of each. Tu Mu reminds us of Han Hsin's
famous reply to the first Han Emperor, who said to him, "How large
an army do you think I could lead?" "Not more than 100,000 men, your
Majesty." "And you?" asked the Emperor. "Oh!" he answered, "the more
the better."

———

2. Fighting with a large army under your command is no-
wise different from fighting with a small one: it is merely a
question of instituting signs and signals.

3. To ensure that your whole host may withstand the brunt

of the enemy's attack and remain unshaken—this is effected by manœuvres direct and indirect.

We now come to one of the most interesting parts of Sun Tzu's treatise, the discussion of *chêng* and *ch'i*. As it is by no means easy to grasp the full significance of these two terms, or to render them at all consistently by good English equivalents, it may be as well to tabulate some of the commentators' remarks before proceeding further. . . . Chia Lin: "In presence of the enemy, your troops should be arrayed in normal fashion, but in order to secure victory abnormal manœuvres must be employed." Mei Yao-ch'ên: "*Ch'i* is active, *chêng* is passive; passivity means waiting for an opportunity, activity brings the victory itself."

Ho Shih: "We must cause the enemy to regard our straightforward attack as one that is secretly designed, and vice versa; thus *chêng* may also be *ch'i*, and *ch'i* may also be *chêng*." He instances the famous exploit of Han Hsin, who when marching ostensibly against Lin-chin, suddenly threw a large force across the Yellow River in wooden tubs, utterly disconcerting his opponent. Here, we are told, the march on Lin-chin was *chêng*, and the surprise manœuvre was *ch'i*. . . .

A comment of the T'ang Emperor T'ai Tsung goes to the root of the matter: ". . . The whole secret lies in confusing the enemy, so that he cannot fathom our real intent." To put it perhaps a little more clearly: any attack or other operation is *chêng*, on which the enemy has had his attention fixed; whereas that is *ch'i*, which takes him by surprise or comes from an unexpected quarter. If the enemy perceives a movement which is meant to be *ch'i*, it immediately becomes *chêng*.

---

4. That the impact of your army may be like a grindstone dashed against an egg—this is effected by the science of weak points and strong.

5. In all fighting, the direct method may be used for joining battle, but indirect methods will be needed in order to secure victory.

Chang Yü says: "Steadily develop indirect tactics, either by pounding the enemy's flanks or falling on his rear." A brilliant example of "indirect tactics" which decided the fortunes of a campaign was Lord Roberts' night march round the Peiwar Kotal in the second Afghan war.

---

6. Indirect tactics, efficiently applied, are inexhaustible as Heaven and Earth, unending as the flow of rivers and streams;

like the sun and moon, they end but to begin anew; like the
four seasons, they pass away but to return once more.

Here we simply have an expression, in figurative language, of the almost
infinite resource of a great leader.

------

7. There are not more than five musical notes, yet the combinations of these five give rise to more melodies than can ever
be heard.

8. There are not more than five primary colours, yet in
combination they produce more hues than can ever be seen.

9. There are not more than five cardinal tastes, yet combinations of them yield more flavours than can ever be tasted.

10. In battle, there are not more than two methods of attack—the direct and the indirect; yet these two in combination
give rise to an endless series of manœuvers.

11. The direct and the indirect lead on to each other in turn.
It is like moving in a circle—you never come to an end. Who
can exhaust the possibilities of their combination?

12. The onset of troops is like the rush of a torrent which
will even roll stones along in its course.

13. The quality of decision is like the well-timed swoop of
a falcon which enables it to strike and destroy its victim.

As applied to the falcon, [this quality] seems to me to denote that in-
stinct of *self-restraint* which keeps the bird from swooping on its quarry
until the right moment, together with the power of judging when the
right moment has arrived. The analogous quality in soldiers is the
highly important one of being able to reserve their fire until the very
instant at which it will be most effective. When the "Victory" went into
action at Trafalgar at hardly more than drifting pace, she was for several minutes exposed to a storm of shot and shell before replying with
a single gun. Nelson coolly waited until he was within close range,
when the broadside he brought to bear worked fearful havoc on the enemy's nearest ships.

------

14. Therefore the good fighter will be terrible in his onset,
and prompt in his decision.

Wang Hsi's note . . . : "This is just how the 'psychological moment'
ought to be seized in war."

------

15. Energy may be likened to the bending of a crossbow; decision, to the releasing of the trigger.

16. Amid the turmoil and tumult of battle, there may be seeming disorder and yet no real disorder at all; amid confusion and chaos, your array may be without head or tail, yet it will be proof against defeat.

Mei Yao-ch'ên says: "The subdivisions of the army having been previously fixed, and the various signals agreed upon, the separating and joining, the dispersing and collecting which will take place in the course of a battle, may give the appearance of disorder when no real disorder is possible. Your formation may be without head or tail, your dispositions all topsy-turvy, and yet a rout of your forces quite out of the question."

17. Simulated disorder postulates perfect discipline; simulated fear postulates courage; simulated weakness postulates strength.

Tu Mu . . . put it quite plainly: "If you wish to feign confusion in order to lure the enemy on, you must first have perfect discipline; if you wish to display timidity in order to entrap the enemy, you must have extreme courage; if you wish to parade your weakness in order to make the enemy over-confident, you must have exceeding strength."

18. Hiding order beneath the cloak of disorder is simply a question of subdivision; concealing courage under a show of timidity presupposes a fund of latent energy; masking strength with weakness is to be effected by tactical dispositions.

Chang Yü relates the following anecdote of Kao Tsu, the first Han Emperor: "Wishing to crush the Hsiung-nu, he sent out spies to report on their condition. But the Hsiung-nu, forewarned, carefully concealed all their able-bodied men and well-fed horses, and only allowed infirm soldiers and emaciated cattle to be seen. The result was that the spies one and all recommended the Emperor to deliver his attack. Lou Ching alone opposed them, saying: 'When two countries go to war, they are naturally inclined to make an ostentatious display of their strength. Yet our spies have seen nothing but old age and infirmity. This is surely some *ruse* on the part of the enemy, and it would be unwise for us to attack.' The Emperor, however, disregarding this advice, fell into the trap and found himself surrounded at Po-têng."

19. Thus one who is skilful at keeping the enemy on the move maintains deceitful appearances, according to which the enemy will act.

Tu Mu ... points out ... : "If our force happens to be superior to the enemy's, weakness may be simulated in order to lure him on; but if inferior, he must be led to believe that we are strong, in order that he may keep off. In fact, all the enemy's movements should be determined by the signs that we choose to give him." [Note this] anecdote of Sun Pin, a descendant of Sun Wu ... : In 341 B.C., the Ch'i State being at war with Wei, sent T'ien Chi and Sun Pin against the general P'ang Chüan, who happened to be a deadly personal enemy of the latter. Sun Pin said: "The Ch'i State has a reputation for cowardice, and therefore our adversary despises us. Let us turn this circumstance to account." Accordingly, when the army had crossed the border into Wei territory, he gave orders to show 100,000 fires on the first night, 50,000 on the next, and the night after only 20,000. P'ang Chüan pursued them hotly, saying to himself: "I knew these men of Ch'i were cowards: their numbers have already fallen away by more than half."

In his retreat, Sun Pin came to a narrow defile, which he calculated that his pursuers would reach after dark. Here he had a tree stripped of its bark, and inscribed upon it the words: "Under this tree shall P'ang Chüan die." Then, as night began to fall, he placed a strong body of archers in ambush near by, with orders to shoot directly they saw a light. Later on, P'ang Chüan arrived at the spot, and noticing the tree, struck a light in order to read what was written on it. His body was immediately riddled by a volley of arrows, and his whole army thrown into confusion.

He sacrifices something, that the enemy may snatch at it.

20. By holding out baits, he keeps him on the march; then with a body of picked men he lies in wait for him.

21. The clever combatant looks to the effect of combined energy, and does not require too much from individuals.

Tu Mu says: "He first of all considers the power of his army in the bulk; afterwards he takes individual talent into account, and uses each man according to his capabilities. He does not demand perfection from the untalented."

Hence his ability to pick out the right men and to utilise combined energy.

22. When he utilises combined energy, his fighting men become as it were like unto rolling logs or stones. For it is the nature of a log or stone to remain motionless on level ground, and to move when on a slope; if four-cornered, to come to a standstill, but if round-shaped, to go rolling down.

23. Thus the energy developed by good fighting men is as the momentum of a round stone rolled down a mountain thousands of feet in height. So much on the subject of energy.

The chief lesson of this chapter, in Tu Mu's opinion, is the paramount importance in war of rapid evolutions and sudden rushes. "Great results," he adds, "can thus be achieved with small forces."

虛 實 篇

VI.

WEAK POINTS AND STRONG

———⟨⟩———

Troops are (or should be) trained to exploit their dominant weapon's strong points. . . . War is a chess game in which both the value of the pieces and the nature of their possible moves vary both with the training of the pieces and the skill of the individual player.

    Theodore Ropp, paraphrasing Von Clausewitz, in *War in the Modern World* (1959)

◆ ◆ ◆

Chang Yü attempts to explain the sequence of chapters as follows: "Chapter IV, on Tactical Dispositions, treated of the offensive and the defensive; chapter V, on Energy, dealt with direct and indirect methods. The good general acquaints himself first with the theory of attack and defence, and then turns his attention to direct and indirect methods. He studies the art of varying and combining these two methods before proceeding to the subject of weak and strong points. For the use of direct or indirect methods arises out of attack and defence, and the perception of weak and strong points depends again on the above methods. Hence the present chapter comes immediately after the chapter on Energy."

————

    1. Sun Tzu said: Whoever is first in the field and awaits the coming of the enemy, will be fresh for the fight; whoever is

second in the field and has to hasten to battle, will arrive exhausted.

2. Therefore the clever combatant imposes his will on the enemy, but does not allow the enemy's will to be imposed upon him.

One mark of a great soldier is that he fights on his own terms or fights not at all.

---

3. By holding out advantages to him, he can cause the enemy to approach of his own accord; or, by inflicting damage, he can make it impossible for the enemy to draw near.

In the first case, he will entice him with a bait; in the second, he will strike at some important point which the enemy will have to defend.

---

4. If the enemy is taking his ease, he can harass him; if well supplied with food, he can starve him out; if quietly encamped, he can force him to move.

The king who is endowed with personality and the material constituents of sovereignty and on whom all right policy rests is called the conqueror. That which encircles him on all sides and prevails in the territory immediately adjacent to his is . . . known as the enemy. . . . A neighboring prince having the fullest measure of antagonism is an enemy. When he is in difficulty, he should be attacked; when he is without support or has weak support, he should be exterminated. In contrary circumstances [when he is strong or has strong support], he should be harassed or weakened.

Kautilya, *Artha Sastra* (fourth or third century B.C.)

---

5. Appear at points which the enemy must hasten to defend; march swiftly to places where you are not expected.

6. An army may march great distances without distress, if it marches through country where the enemy is not.

Ts'ao Kung sums up very well: "Emerge from the void, strike at vulnerable points, shun places that are defended, attack in unexpected quarters."

---

7. You can be sure of succeeding in your attacks if you only attack places which are undefended.

Wang Hsi rightly explains ["undefended"] as "weak points; that is to say, where the general is lacking in capacity, or the soldiers in spirit; where the walls are not strong enough, or the precautions not strict enough; where relief comes too late, or provisions are too scanty, or the defenders are [at] variance amongst themselves."

You can ensure the safety of your defence if you only hold positions that cannot be attacked.

I.e., where there are none of the weak points mentioned above.... Chang Yü [says]: "He who is skilled in attack flashes forth from the topmost heights of heaven, making it impossible for the enemy to guard against him. This being so, the places that I shall attack are precisely those that the enemy cannot defend ... He who is skilled in defence hides in the most secret recesses of the earth, making it impossible for the enemy to estimate his whereabouts. This being so, the places that I shall hold are precisely those that the enemy cannot attack."

Viewers of films such as Ang Lee's *Crouching Tiger, Hidden Dragon* (2000) or the kung-fu films of Jackie Chan will recognize the imagery. It is also strongly present, of course, in martial arts disciplines such as tai chi.   DG

8. Hence that general is skilful in attack whose opponent does not know what to defend; and he is skilful in defence whose opponent does not know what to attack.

An aphorism which puts the whole art of war into a nutshell.

9. O divine art of subtlety and secrecy! Through you we learn to be invisible, through you inaudible; and hence we can hold the enemy's fate in our hands.

It was an extraordinary achievement of modern warfare: between 12 and 25 October, 1950, the intelligence staffs of MacArthur's armies failed to discern the slightest evidence of the movement of 130,000 soldiers and porters. A combination of superb fieldcraft and camouflage by the Chinese, with their lack of use of any of

the conventional means of detecting modern military movement—
wireless traffic, mechanised activity, supply dumps—blinded the
U.N. High Command to what was taking place on its front.

    Max Hastings, *The Korean War,* 1987

———————

10. You may advance and be absolutely irresistible, if you
make for the enemy's weak points; you may retire and be safe
from pursuit if your movements are more rapid than those of
the enemy.

Mao is the surgeon, exploring the wound, insisting above everything else on the delicate probing, the discovery of the enemy's
weakened nerve, the dangerous point where weakness is balanced
by strength: at this point, he will order attack.

    Robert Payne, *Mao Tse-tung* (1969)

———————

11. If we wish to fight, the enemy can be forced to an engagement even though he be sheltered behind a high rampart
and a deep ditch. All we need do is to attack some other place
that he will be obliged to relieve.

Tu Mu says: "If the enemy is the invading party, we can cut his line of
communications and occupy the roads by which he will have to return;
if we are the invaders, we may direct our attack against the sovereign
himself." It is clear that Sun Tzu, unlike certain generals in the late Boer
war, was no believer in frontal attacks.

———————

12. If we do not wish to fight, we can prevent the enemy
from engaging us even though the lines of our encampment be
merely traced out on the ground. All we need do is to throw
something odd and unaccountable in his way.

Tu Mu [illustrates this with an anecdote] of Chu-ko Liang, who when
occupying Yang-p'ing and about to be attacked by Ssu-ma I, suddenly
struck his colours, stopped the beating of the drums, and flung open the
city gates, showing only a few men engaged in sweeping and sprinkling
the ground. This unexpected proceeding had the intended effect; for
Ssu-ma I, suspecting an ambush, actually drew off his army and re-
treated. What Sun Tzu is advocating here, therefore, is nothing more
nor less than the timely use of "bluff."

———————

13. By discovering the enemy's dispositions and remaining invisible ourselves, we can keep our forces concentrated, while the enemy's must be divided.

The conclusion is perhaps not very obvious, but Chang Yü (after Mei Yao-ch'ên) rightly explains it thus: "If the enemy's dispositions are visible, we can make for him in one body; whereas, our own dispositions being kept secret, the enemy will be obliged to divide his forces in order to guard against attack from every quarter."

14. We can form a single united body, while the enemy must split up into fractions. Hence there will be a whole pitted against separate parts of a whole, which means that we shall be many to the enemy's few.

15. And if we are able thus to attack an inferior force with a superior one, our opponents will be in dire straits.

16. The spot where we intend to fight must not be made known; for then the enemy will have to prepare against a possible attack at several different points;

Sheridan once explained the reason of General Grant's victories by saying that "while his opponents were kept fully employed wondering what he was going to do, *he* was thinking most of what he was going to do himself."

and his forces being thus distributed in many directions, the numbers we shall have to face at any given point will be proportionately few.

17. For should the enemy strengthen his van, he will weaken his rear; should he strengthen his rear, he will weaken his van; should he strengthen his left, he will weaken his right; should he strengthen his right, he will weaken his left. If he sends reinforcements everywhere, he will everywhere be weak.

In Frederick the Great's *Instructions to his Generals* we read: "A defensive war is apt to betray us into too frequent detachment. Those generals who have had but little experience attempt to protect every point, while those who are better acquainted with their profession, having only the capital object in view, guard against a decisive blow, and acquiesce in smaller misfortunes to avoid greater."

18. Numerical weakness comes from having to prepare against possible attacks; numerical strength, from compelling our adversary to make these preparations against us.

The highest generalship, in Col. Henderson's words, is "to compel the enemy to disperse his army, and then to concentrate superior force against each fraction in turn."

———————

19. Knowing the place and the time of the coming battle, we may concentrate from the greatest distances in order to fight.

What Sun Tzu evidently has in mind is that nice calculation of distances and that masterly employment of strategy which enable a general to divide his army for the purpose of a long and rapid march, and afterwards to effect a junction at precisely the right spot and the right hour in order to confront the enemy in overwhelming strength. Among many such successful junctions which military history records, one of the most dramatic and decisive was the appearance of Blücher just at the critical moment on the field of Waterloo.

———————

Gebhard Leberecht von Blücher (1742–1819) was a daring, highly decorated, and famously hard-living, hard-fighting Prussian cavalry officer. He beat Napoleon I on several occasions and was commander-in-chief of the armies when they marched on Paris and brought down the First Empire. When Napoleon regained power, von Blücher, now a prince and an old man, was put in command of the Army of the Rhine. Badly wounded in battle at Ligny, von Blücher nevertheless led his troops on a long and brutal march to join Wellington at Waterloo. His army's crushing intervention was decisive.   DG

———————

20. But if neither time nor place be known, then the left wing will be impotent to succour the right, the right equally impotent to succour the left, the van unable to relieve the rear, or the rear to support the van. How much more so if the furthest portions of the army are anything under a hundred *li* apart, and even the nearest are separated by several *li*!

The Chinese of this last sentence is a little lacking in precision, but the mental picture we are required to draw is probably that of an army advancing towards a given rendez-vous in separate columns, each of which has orders to be there on a fixed date. If the general allows the various detachments to proceed at haphazard, without precise instructions as to the time and place of meeting, the enemy will be able to annihilate the army in detail. Chang Yü's note may be worth quoting here: "If we do not know the place where our opponents mean to concentrate or the day on which they will join battle, our unity will be forfeited through our preparations for defence, and the positions we hold will be insecure. Suddenly happening upon a powerful foe, we shall be brought to battle in a flurried condition, and no mutual support will be possible between wings, vanguard or rear, especially if there is any great distance between the foremost and hindmost divisions of the army."

Let no act be done at haphazard, nor otherwise than according to the finished rules that govern its kind.

Marcus Aurelius, *Meditations* (A.D. 167)

-----

21. Though according to my estimate the soldiers of Yüeh exceed our own in number, that shall advantage them nothing in the matter of victory. I say then that victory can be achieved.

Alas for these brave words! The long feud between the two states [Wu and Yüeh] ended in 473 B.C. with the total defeat of Wu by Kou Chien and its incorporation in Yüeh. This was doubtless long after Sun Tzu's death. . . . Chang Yü is the only one to point out the seeming discrepancy [between chapter IV, paragraph 4, and this], which he thus goes on to explain: "In the chapter on Tactical Dispositions it is said: 'One may *know* how to conquer without being able to *do* it,' whereas here we have the statement that 'victory can be achieved.' The explanation is, that in the former chapter, where the offensive and defensive are under discussion, it is said that if the enemy is fully prepared, one cannot make certain of beating him. But the present passage refers particularly to the soldiers of Yüeh who, according to Sun Tzu's calculations, will be kept in ignorance of the time and place of the impending struggle. That is why he says here that victory can be achieved."

-----

22. Though the enemy be stronger in numbers, we may prevent him from fighting. Scheme so as to discover his plans and the likelihood of their success.

23. Rouse him, and learn the principle of his activity or inactivity. Force him to reveal himself, so as to find out his vulnerable spots.

24. Carefully compare the opposing army with your own, so that you may know where strength is superabundant and where it is deficient.

25. In making tactical dispositions, the highest pitch you can attain is to conceal them; conceal your dispositions, and you will be safe from the prying of the subtlest spies, from the machinations of the wisest brains.

26. How victory may be produced for them out of the enemy's own tactics—that is what the multitude cannot comprehend.

27. All men can see the tactics whereby I conquer, but what none can see is the strategy out of which victory is evolved.

I.e., everybody can see superficially how a battle is won; what they cannot see is the long series of plans and combinations which has preceded the battle.

———

28. Do not repeat the tactics which have gained you one victory, but let your methods be regulated by the infinite variety of circumstances.

As Wang Hsi sagely remarks: "There is but one root-principle underlying victory, but the tactics which lead up to it are infinite in number." With this compare Col. Henderson [writing about Stonewall Jackson]: "The rules of strategy are few and simple. They may be learned in a week. They may be taught by familiar illustrations or a dozen diagrams. But such knowledge will no more teach a man to lead an army like Napoleon than a knowledge of grammar will teach him to write like Gibbon."

———

29. Military tactics are like unto water; for water in its natural course runs away from high places and hastens downwards.

30. So in war, the way is to avoid what is strong and to strike at what is weak.

Like water, taking the line of least resistance.

———

31. Water shapes its course according to the nature of the ground over which it flows; the soldier works out his victory in relation to the foe whom he is facing.

32. Therefore, just as water retains no constant shape, so in warfare there are no constant conditions.

33. He who can modify his tactics in relation to his opponent and thereby succeed in winning, may be called a heaven-born captain.

34. The five elements

Water, fire, wood, metal, earth.

---

are not always equally predominant;

That is, as Wang Hsi says: "They predominate alternately."

---

the four seasons make way for each other in turn. There are short days and long; the moon has its periods of waning and waxing.

The purport of the passage is simply to illustrate the want of fixity in war by the changes constantly taking place in Nature. The comparison is not very happy, however, because the regularity of the phenomena which Sun Tzu mentions is by no means paralleled in war.

VII.

MANŒUVRING

In war, three-quarters turns on personal character and relations; the balance of manpower and materials counts only for the remaining quarter.

Napoleon I, "Observations sur les affaires d'Espagne" (1808)

✦ ✦ ✦

1. Sun Tzu said: In war, the general receives his commands from the sovereign.

2. Having collected an army and concentrated his forces, he must blend and harmonise the different elements thereof before pitching his camp.

3. After that, comes tactical manœuvring, than which there is nothing more difficult.

I have departed slightly from the traditional interpretation of Ts'ao Kung, who says: "From the time of receiving the sovereign's instructions until our encampment over against the enemy, the tactics to be pursued are most difficult." It seems to me that the tactics or manœuvres can hardly be said to begin until the army has sallied forth and encamped, and Ch'ên Hao's note gives colour to this view: "For levying, concentrating, harmonising and intrenching an army, there are plenty of old rules which will serve. The real difficulty comes when we engage in tactical operations." Tu Yu also observes that "the great difficulty is to be beforehand with the enemy in seizing favourable positions."

The difficulty of tactical manœuvring consists in turning the
devious into the direct, and misfortune into gain.

This is one of those highly condensed and somewhat enigmatical expressions of which Sun Tzu is so fond. This is how it is explained by
Ts'ao Kung: "Make it appear that you are a long way off, then cover
the distance rapidly and arrive on the scene before your opponent." Tu
Mu says: "Hoodwink the enemy, so that he may be remiss and leisurely
while you are dashing along with the utmost speed." Ho Shih gives a
slightly different turn to the sentence: "Although you may have difficult
ground to traverse and natural obstacles to encounter, this is a drawback
which can be turned into actual advantage by celerity of movement."
Signal examples of this saying are afforded by the two famous passages
across the Alps—that of Hannibal, which laid Italy at his mercy, and
that of Napoleon two thousand years later, which resulted in the great
victory of Marengo.

----

4. Thus, to take a long and circuitous route, after enticing
the enemy out of the way, and though starting after him, to
contrive to reach the goal before him, shows knowledge of the
artifice of *deviation*.

Chia Lin [says]: "If our adversary's course is really a short one, and we
can manage to divert him from it, either by simulating weakness or by
holding out some small advantage, we shall be able to beat him in the
race for good positions." This is quite a defensible view, though not
adopted by any other commentator. . . .
    Tu Mu cites the famous march of Chao Shê in 270 B.C. to relieve
the town of O-yü, which was [under siege] by a Ch'in army. The King
of Chao first consulted Lien P'o on the advisability of attempting a relief,
but the latter thought the distance too great, and the intervening country
too rugged and difficult. His majesty then turned to Chao Shê, who fully
admitted the hazardous nature of the march, but finally said: "We shall
be like two rats fighting in a hole—and the pluckier one will win!" So
he left the capital with his army, but had only gone a distance of 30 *li*
when he stopped and began throwing up intrenchments. For 28 days he
continued strengthening his fortifications, and took care that spies
should carry the intelligence to the enemy.
    The Ch'in general was overjoyed, and attributed his adversary's tar-
diness to the fact that the beleaguered city was in the Han State, and

thus not actually part of Chao territory. But the spies had no sooner departed than Chao Shê began a forced march lasting for two days and one night, and arrived on the scene of action with such astonishing rapidity that he was able to occupy a commanding position on the "North hill" before the enemy had got wind of his movements. A crushing defeat followed for the Ch'in forces, who were obliged to raise the siege of O-yü in all haste and retreat across the border.

_____

5. Manœuvring with an army is advantageous; with an undisciplined multitude, most dangerous.

6. If you set a fully equipped army in march in order to snatch an advantage, the chances are that you will be too late. On the other hand, to detach a flying column for the purpose involves the sacrifice of its baggage and stores.

I submit my own rendering [of this passage] without much enthusiasm, being convinced that there is some deep-seated corruption in the text. On the whole, it is clear that Sun Tzu does not approve of a lengthy march being undertaken without supplies.

_____

7. Thus, if you order your men to roll up their buff-coats,

Chang Yü says: "This means, in full panoply."

_____

and make forced marches without halting day or night, covering double the usual distance at a stretch,

The ordinary day's march, according to Tu Mu, was 30 _li_; but on one occasion, when pursuing Liu Pei, Ts'ao Ts'ao is said to have covered the incredible distance of 300 _li_ within twenty-four hours.

_____

doing a hundred _li_ in order to wrest an advantage, the leaders of all your three divisions will fall into the hands of the enemy.

8. The stronger men will be in front, the jaded ones will fall behind, and on this plan only one-tenth of your army will reach its destination.

The moral is, as Ts'ao Kung and others point out: Don't march a hundred _li_ to gain a tactical advantage, either with or without impedimenta. Manœuvres of this description should be confined to short distances.

Stonewall Jackson said: "The hardships of forced marches are often more painful than the dangers of battle." He did not often call upon his troops for extraordinary exertions. It was only when he intended a surprise, or when a rapid retreat was imperative, that he sacrificed everything to speed.

---

9. If you march fifty *li* in order to outmanœuvre the enemy, you will lose the leader of your first division, and only half your force will reach the goal.

Literally, "the leader of the first division will be *torn away*." [From the *Tso Chuan*, 19th year:] "This is a case of [the falling tree] tearing up its roots."

Like so many texts in a literature as vast and ancient as China's, the reference to the *Tso chuan* comes with a step-ladder provenance and mysteries of its own. The *Tso chuan*—the *Tso Commentary on the Spring and Autumn Annals*—existed by the early Han Dynasty. When precisely is open to question, but its import is unquestionable.

Chinese intellectual activity, from poetry to military tracts, builds upon references to a long intellectual past, especially to what are known as the *Five Classics*. Consequently, idioms and points of reference can transmit encyclopedic layers of meaning in astonishingly brief lines. Along with the *Kung-yung* and the *Ku-liang* commentaries, the *Tso chuan* sets out to explain the background and significance of the events related in the fifth of the great Five Classics, the *Ch'un-Ch'iu*, or the *Spring and Autumn Annals*. Employing extremely laconic language, it chronicles events in the state of Lu from 722 to 481 B.C. The *Annals* were essential study for China's educated classes across the millennia. Asian scholar William Theodore de Bary notes that they were regarded "not only as the final authority upon questions of ancient history . . . but as the embodiment of moral law . . . and the source of all wisdom and right knowledge." Therefore, any reference to the Classics or to the commentaries on them is the same as citing the final authority on a subject.   DG

---

10. If you march thirty *li* with the same object, two-thirds of your army will arrive.

In the *T'ung Tien* [Tu Yu's encyclopedic treatise on the Constitution] is added: "From this we may know the difficulty of manœuvring."

---

11. We may take it then that an army without its baggage-train is lost; without provisions it is lost; without bases of supply it is lost.

This is explained by Tu Yu as "fodder and the like"; by Tu Mu and Chang Yü as "goods in general"; and by Wang Hsi as "fuel, salt, food-stuffs, etc." But I think what Sun Tzu meant was "stores and accumulated in dépôts," as distinguished from … the various impedimenta accompanying an army on its march.

———————

12. We cannot enter into alliances until we are acquainted with the designs of our neighbours.

13. We are not fit to lead an army on the march unless we are familiar with the face of the country—its mountains and forests, its pitfalls and precipices, its marshes and swamps.

14. We shall be unable to turn natural advantages to account unless we make use of local guides.

15. In war, practise dissimulation, and you will succeed. Move only if there is a real advantage to be gained.

16. Whether to concentrate or to divide your troops, must be decided by circumstances.

17. Let your rapidity be that of the wind,

The simile is doubly appropriate, because the wind is not only swift but, as Mei Yao-ch'ên points out, "invisible and leaves no tracks."

———————

your compactness that of the forest.

Mêng Shih [notes]: "When slowly marching, order and ranks must be preserved"—so as to guard against surprise attacks. But natural forests do not grow in rows, whereas they do generally possess the quality of density or compactness.

———————

18. In raiding and plundering be like fire, in immovability like a mountain.

That is [with reference to the latter], when holding a position from which the enemy is trying to dislodge you, or perhaps, as Tu Yu says, when he is trying to entice you into a trap.

———————

19. Let your plans be dark and impenetrable as night, and when you move, fall like a thunderbolt.

Tu Yu quotes a saying of T'ai Kung which has passed into a proverb: "You cannot shut your ears to the thunder or your eyes to the lightning—so rapid are they." Likewise, an attack should be made so quickly that it cannot be parried.

———

20. When you plunder a countryside, let the spoil be divided amongst your men;

Sun Tzu wishes to lessen the abuses of indiscriminate plundering by insisting that all booty shall be thrown into a common stock, which may afterwards be fairly divided amongst all.

———

when you capture new territory, cut it up into allotments for the benefit of the soldiery.

Ch'ên Hao also says: "Quarter your soldiers on the land, and let them sow and plant it." It is by acting on this principle, and harvesting the lands they invaded, that the Chinese have succeeded in carrying out some of their most memorable and triumphant expeditions, such as that of Pan Ch'ao, who penetrated to the Caspian Sea.

———

21. Ponder and deliberate

Note that both these words [in English and in Chinese] are really metaphors derived from the use of scales.

———

before you make a move.

Chang Yü quotes [another commentator] as saying that we must not break camp until we have gauged the resisting power of the enemy and the cleverness of the opposing general.

———

22. He will conquer who has learnt the artifice of deviation. Such is the art of manœuvring.

With these words, the chapter would naturally come to an end. But there now follows a long appendix in the shape of an extract from an earlier book on War, now lost, but apparently extant at the time when Sun Tzu wrote. The style of this fragment is not noticeably different from that of Sun Tzu himself, but no commentator raises a doubt as to its genuineness.

***

23. The Book of Army Management says:

It is perhaps significant that none of the earlier commentators give us any information about this work. Mei Yao-Ch'ên calls it "an ancient military classic," and Wang Hsi, "an old book on war." Considering the enormous amount of fighting that had gone on for centuries before Sun Tzu's time between the various kingdoms and principalities of China, it is not in itself improbable that a collection of military maxims should have been made and written down at some earlier period.

***

On the field of battle, the spoken word does not carry far enough: hence the institution of gongs and drums. Nor can ordinary objects be seen clearly enough: hence the institution of banners and flags.

24. Gongs and drums, banners and flags, are means whereby the ears and eyes of the host may be focussed on one particular point.

Chang Yü says: "If sight and hearing converge simultaneously on the same object, the evolutions of as many as a million soldiers will be like those of a single man!"

***

25. The host thus forming a single united body, it is impossible either for the brave to advance alone, or for the cowardly to retreat alone.

Chang Yü quotes a saying: "Equally guilty are those who advance against orders and those who retreat against orders." Tu Mu tells a story in this connection of Wu Ch'i, when he was fighting against the Ch'in State. Before the battle had begun, one of his soldiers, a man of matchless daring, sallied forth by himself, captured two heads from the enemy, and returned to camp. Wu Ch'i had the man instantly executed, whereupon an officer ventured to remonstrate, saying; "This man was a good soldier, and ought not to have been beheaded." Wu Ch'i replied, "I fully believe he was a good soldier, but I had him beheaded because he acted without orders."

This is the art of handling large masses of men.

26. In night-fighting, then, make much use of signal-fires and drums, and in fighting by day, of flags and banners, as a means of influencing the ears and eyes of your army.

Ch'ên Hao alludes to Li Kuang-pi's night ride to Ho-yang at the head of 500 mounted men [c.760 A.D.]; they made such an imposing display with torches, that though the rebel leader Shih Ssü-ming had a large army, he did not dare to dispute their passage.

---

27. A whole army may be robbed of its spirit;

"In war," says Chang Yü, "if a spirit of anger can be made to pervade all ranks of an army at one and the same time, its onset will be irresistible. Now the spirit of the enemy's soldiers will be keenest when they have newly arrived on the scene, and it is therefore our cue not to fight at once, but to wait until their ardour and enthusiasm have worn off, and then strike. It is in this way that they may be robbed of their keen spirit."

Li Ch'üan and others tell an anecdote [in the *Tso Chuan*] of Ts'ao Kuei, a protégé of Duke Chuang of Lu. The latter State was attacked by Ch'i, and the Duke was about to join battle at Ch'ang-cho, after the first roll of the enemy's drums, when Ts'ao said, "Not just yet." Only after their drums had beaten for the third time, did he give the word for attack. Then they fought, and the men of Ch'i were utterly defeated. Questioned afterwards by the Duke as to the meaning of his delay, Ts'ao Kuei replied, "In battle, a courageous spirit is everything. Now the first roll of the drum tends to create this spirit, but with the second it is already on the wane, and after the third it is gone altogether. I attacked when their spirit was gone and ours was at its height. Hence our victory." [The writer Wu Tzu] puts "spirit" first among the "four important influences" in war, and continues: "The value of a whole army—a mighty host of a million men—is dependent on one man alone: Such is the influence of spirit!"

---

a commander-in-chief may be robbed of his presence of mind.

Chang Yü says: "Presence of mind is the general's most important asset. It is the quality which enables him to discipline disorder and to inspire courage into the panic-stricken." The great general Li Ching (A.D. 571–649) has a saying: "Attacking does not merely consist in assaulting walled cities or striking at an army in battle array; it must include the art of assailing the enemy's mental equilibrium."

Intellect and education play a more prominent part in war than stamina and courage.

George Francis Robert Henderson and Sir Thomas Barclay, "War," *Encyclopedia Britannica*, eleventh edition (1910)

28. Now a soldier's spirit is keenest in the morning;

Always provided, I suppose, that he has had breakfast. At the battle of the Trebia, the Romans were foolishly allowed to fight fasting, whereas Hannibal's men had breakfasted at their leisure.

by noonday it has begun to flag; and in the evening, his mind is bent only on returning to camp.

29. A clever general, therefore, avoids an army when its spirit is keen, but attacks it when it is sluggish and inclined to return. This is the art of studying moods.

30. Disciplined and calm, to await the appearance of disorder and hubbub amongst the enemy:—this is the art of retaining self-possession.

31. To be near the goal while the enemy is still far from it, to wait at ease while the enemy is toiling and struggling, to be well-fed while the enemy is famished:—this is the art of husbanding one's strength.

32. To refrain from intercepting an enemy whose banners are in perfect order, to refrain from attacking an army drawn up in calm and confident array:—this is the art of studying circumstances.

33. It is a military axiom not to advance uphill against the enemy, nor to oppose him when he comes downhill.

34. Do not pursue an enemy who simulates flight; do not attack soldiers whose temper is keen.

35. Do not swallow a bait offered by the enemy. Do not interfere with an army that is returning home.

The commentators explain [the latter] piece of advice by saying that a man whose heart is set on returning home will fight to the death against any attempt to bar his way, and is therefore too dangerous an opponent to be tackled. Chang Yü quotes the words of Han Hsin: "Invincible is the soldier who hath his desire and returneth homewards." A marvellous tale is told of Ts'ao Ts'ao's courage and resource . . . : In 198 A.D., he was besieging Chang Hsiu in Jang, when Liu Piao sent reinforcements with a view to cutting off Ts'ao's retreat. The latter was obliged to draw off his troops, only to find himself hemmed in between two enemies, who were guarding each outlet of a narrow pass in which he had engaged himself.

In this desperate plight, Ts'ao waited until nightfall, when he bored a tunnel into the mountain side and laid an ambush in it. Then he marched on with his baggage-train, and when it grew light, Chang Hsiu, finding that the bird had flown, pressed after him in hot pursuit. As soon as the whole army had passed by, the hidden troops fell on its rear, while Ts'ao himself turned and met his pursuers in front, so that they were thrown into confusion and annihilated. Ts'ao Ts'ao said afterwards, "The brigands tried to check my army in its retreat and brought me to battle in a desperate position; hence I knew how to overcome them."

---

36. When you surround an army, leave an outlet free.

This does not mean that the enemy is to be allowed to escape. The object, as Tu Mu puts it, is "to make him believe that there is a road to safety, and thus prevent his fighting with the courage of despair." Tu Mu adds pleasantly: "After that, you may crush him."

Do not press a desperate foe too hard.

Ch'ên Hao quotes the saying, "Birds and beasts when brought to bay will use their claws and teeth." Chang Yü says: "If your adversary has burned his boats and destroyed his cooking-pots, and is ready to stake all on the issue of a battle, he must not be pushed to extremities." . . .

Ho Shih illustrates the meaning by a story taken from the life of Fu Yen-Ch'ing. . . . That general, together with his colleague Tu Chung-wei, was surrounded by a vastly superior army of Khitans in the year 945 A.D. The country was bare and desert-like, and the little Chinese force was soon in dire straits for want of water. The wells they bored ran dry, and the men were reduced to squeezing lumps of mud and sucking out the moisture. Their ranks thinned rapidly, until at last Fu Yen-Ch'ing exclaimed, "We are desperate men. Far better to die for our country than to go with fettered hands into captivity!"

A strong gale happened to be blowing from the northeast and darkening the air with dense clouds of sandy dust. Tu Chung-wei was for waiting until this had abated before deciding on a final attack; but luckily another officer, Li Shou-chêng by name, was quicker to see an opportunity, and said: "They are many and we are few, but in the midst of this sandstorm our numbers will not be discernible; victory will go to the strenuous fighter, and the wind will be our best ally." Accordingly, Fu Yen-Ch'ing made a sudden and wholly unexpected onslaught with his cavalry, routed the barbarians and succeeded in breaking through to safety.

---

37. Such is the art of warfare.

I take it that these words conclude the extract from the Book of Army Management, which began at paragraph 23.

九 變 篇

VIII.

VARIATION OF TACTICS

There is required for the composition of a great commander not only massive common sense and reasoning power, not only imagination, but also an element of legerdemain, an original and sinister touch, which leaves the enemy puzzled as well as beaten.

Winston Churchill, *The World Crisis* (1923)

✦ ✦ ✦

The heading means literally "The Nine Variations," but, as Sun Tzu does not appear to enumerate these, and as, indeed, he has already told us (chapter V, paragraphs 6–11) that such deflections from the ordinary course are practically innumerable, we have little option but to follow Wang Hsi, who says that "Nine" stands for an indefinitely large number: "All it means is that in warfare we ought to vary our tactics to the utmost degree." . . . The only other alternative is to suppose that something has been lost—a supposition to which the unusual shortness of the chapter lends some weight.

---

1. Sun Tzu said: In war, the general receives his commands from the sovereign, collects his army and concentrates his forces.

Repeated from chapter VII, paragraph 1, where it is certainly more in place. It may have been interpolated here merely in order to supply a beginning to the chapter.

---

2. When in difficult country, do not encamp. In country where high roads intersect, join hands with your allies. Do not linger in dangerously isolated positions.

Chang Yü [defines the last-named situation as being] situated across the frontier, in hostile territory. Li Ch'üan says it is "country in which there are no springs or wells, flocks or herds, vegetables or firewood"; Chia Lin, "one of gorges, chasms and precipices, without a road by which to advance."

───────────

In hemmed-in situations, you must resort to stratagem. In a desperate position, you must fight.

Chang Yü has an important note here. . . . : "The reason why only five [of the nine variations] are given is that the subject is treated *en précis*. . . . All kinds of ground have corresponding military positions, and also a variation of tactics suitable to each. . . . [But] he wishes here to speak of the Five Advantages, so he begins by setting forth the Nine Variations. These are inseparably connected in practice, and therefore they are dealt with together." The weak point of this argument is the suggestion that "five things" can stand as . . . an abstract or abridgment of nine, when those that are omitted are not less important than those that appear, and when one of the latter is not included amongst the nine at all.

───────────

3. There are roads which must not be followed,

"Especially those leading through narrow defiles," says Li Ch'üan, "where an ambush is to be feared."

───────────

armies which must not be attacked,

More correctly, perhaps, "there are times when an army must not be attacked." Ch'ên Hao says: "When you see your way to obtain a trivial advantage, but are powerless to inflict a real defeat, refrain from attacking, for fear of overtaxing your men's strength."

───────────

towns which must not be besieged,

Ts'ao Kung gives an interesting illustration from his own experience. When invading the territory of Hsü-chou, he ignored the city of Hua-pi, which lay directly in his path, and pressed on into the heart of the country. This excellent strategy was rewarded by the subsequent capture of no fewer than fourteen important district cities. Chang Yü says: "No town should be attacked which, if taken, cannot be held, or if left alone, will not cause any trouble." Hsün Ying, when urged to attack Pi-yang, replied: "The city is small and well-fortified; even if I succeed in taking it, it will be no great feat of arms; whereas if I fail, I shall make myself a laughing-stock."

In the seventeenth century, sieges still formed a large proportion of war. It was [Marshal] Turenne who directed attention to the importance of marches, countermarches and manœuvres. He said: "It is a great mistake to waste men in taking a town when the same expenditure of soldiers will gain a province."

---

positions which must not be contested, commands of the sovereign which must not be obeyed.

This is a hard saying for the Chinese, with their reverence for authority, and Wei Liao Tzu (quoted by Tu Mu) is moved to exclaim: "Weapons are baleful instruments, strife is antagonistic to virtue, a military commander is the negation of civil order!" The unpalatable fact remains, however, that even Imperial wishes must be subordinated to military necessity.

> I've always taken it for granted that the Führer left the command of the army to me. This crazy order has come like a bombshell. He can't just blindly apply experience he gained in Russia to the war in Africa. He should have left the decision here to me. . . . Until this moment, we in Africa had always had complete freedom of action. Now that was over. . . . An overwhelming bitterness welled up in us when we saw the superlative spirit of the army, in which every man, from the highest to the lowest, knew that even the greatest effort could no longer change the course of battle.
>
> Field Marshal Rommel, on Adolf Hitler's interference and the German defeat at El Alamein (1942)

---

4. The general who thoroughly understands the advantages that accompany variation of tactics knows how to handle his troops.

5. The general who does not understand these, may be well acquainted with the configuration of the country, yet he will not be able to turn his knowledge to practical account.

Literally, "get the advantage of the ground," which means not only securing good positions, but availing oneself of natural advantages in every possible way. Chang Yü says: "Every kind of ground is characterised by certain natural features, and also gives scope for a certain variability of plan. How is it possible to turn these natural features to account unless topographical knowledge is supplemented by versatility of mind?"

6. So, the student of war who is unversed in the art of varying his plans, even though he be acquainted with the Five Advantages, will fail to make the best use of his men.

Chia Lin . . . tells us that these imply five obvious and generally advantageous lines of action, namely: "If a certain road is short, it must be followed; if an army is isolated, it must be attacked; if a town is in a parlous condition, it must be besieged; if a position can be stormed, it must be attempted; and if consistent with military operations, the ruler's commands must be obeyed." But there are circumstances which sometimes forbid a general to use these advantages.

For instance, "a certain road may be the shortest way for him, but if he knows that it abounds in natural obstacles, or that the enemy has laid an ambush on it, he will not follow that road. A hostile force may be open to attack, but if he knows that it is hard-pressed and likely to fight with desperation, he will refrain from striking," and so on. . . . Hence we see the uselessness of knowing the one without the other—of having an eye for weaknesses in the enemy's armour without being clever enough to recast one's plans on the spur of the moment.

7. Hence in the wise leader's plans, considerations of advantage and of disadvantage will be blended together.

"Whether in an advantageous position or a disadvantageous one," says Ts'ao Kung, "the opposite state should be always present to your mind."

Our strategy is "pit one against ten," and our tactics are "pit ten against one." These contrary and yet complementary propositions constitute one of our principles for gaining mastery over the enemy.

Mao Tse-tung, *Problems of Strategy in China's Revolutionary War* (1936)

8. If our expectation of advantage be tempered in this way, we may succeed in accomplishing the essential part of our schemes.

Tu Mu [says]: "If we wish to wrest an advantage from the enemy, we must not fix our minds on that alone, but allow for the possibility of the enemy also doing some harm to us, and let this enter as a factor into our calculations."

9. If, on the other hand, in the midst of difficulties we are always ready to seize an advantage, we may extricate ourselves from misfortune.

A translator cannot emulate the conciseness of [the original Chinese, which reads, word for word] "to blend [thoughts of advantage] with disadvantage," but the meaning is as given. Tu Mu says: "If I wish to extricate myself from a dangerous position, I must consider not only the enemy's ability to injure me, but also my own ability to gain an advantage over the enemy. If in my counsels these two considerations are properly blended, I shall succeed in liberating myself . . . For instance, if I am surrounded by the enemy and only think of effecting an escape, the nervelessness of my policy will incite my adversary to pursue and crush me; it would be far better to encourage my men to deliver a bold counter-attack, and use the advantage thus gained to free myself from the enemy's toils."

Fortune favors the brave.
    Terence, *Phormio* (c.161 B.C.)

Death is nothing. But to live defeated and without glory, that is to die every day.
    Napoleon I (1804)

10. Reduce the hostile chiefs by inflicting damage on them;

Chia Lin enumerates several ways of inflicting this injury . . . :—"Entice away the enemy's best and wisest men, so that he may be left without counsellors. Introduce traitors into his country, that the government policy may be rendered futile. Foment intrigue and deceit, and thus sow dissension between the ruler and his ministers. By means of every artful

contrivance, cause deterioration amongst his men and waste of his treasure. Corrupt his morals by insidious gifts leading him into excess. Disturb and unsettle his mind by presenting him with lovely women."
Chang Yü (after Wang Hsi) [says]: "Get the enemy . . . into a position
where he must suffer injury, and he will submit of his own accord."

---

make trouble for them, and keep them constantly engaged;

Literally [with reference to the latter phrase], "make servants of them."
Tu Yu says: "Prevent them from having any rest."

---

hold out specious allurements, and make them rush to any
given point.

Mêng Shih's note . . . : "Cause them to forget *pien* (the reasons for acting
otherwise than on their first impulse), and hasten in our direction."

---

11. The art of war teaches us to rely not on the likelihood
of the enemy's not coming, but on our own readiness to receive
him; not on the chance of his not attacking, but rather on the
fact that we have made our position unassailable.

12. There are five dangerous faults which may affect a general: (1) Recklessness, which leads to destruction;

"Bravery without forethought," as Ts'ao Kung analyses it, which causes
a man to fight blindly and desperately like a mad bull. Such an opponent,
says Chang Yü, "must not be encountered with brute force, but may be
lured into an ambush and slain." [Wu Tzu says:] "In estimating the
character of a general, men are wont to pay exclusive attention to his
courage, forgetting that courage is only one out of many qualities which
a general should possess. The merely brave man is prone to fight recklessly; and he who fights recklessly, without any perception of what is
expedient, must be condemned." Ssu-ma Fa, too, makes the incisive re-
mark, "Simply going to one's death does not bring about victory."

---

(2) cowardice, which leads to capture;

Ts'ao Kung [describes the coward as] the man "whom timidity prevents
from advancing to seize an advantage," and Wang Hsi adds, "who is
quick to flee at the sight of danger." Mêng Shih gives the closer para-

phrase "he who is bent on returning alive," that is, the man who will never take a risk. But, as Sun Tzu knew, nothing is to be achieved in war unless you are willing to take risks. T'ai Kung said: "He who lets an advantage slip will subsequently bring upon himself real disaster."

In 404 A.D., Liu Yü pursued the rebel Huan Hsüan up the Yangtsze and fought a naval battle with him at the island of Ch'êng-hung. The loyal troops numbered only a few thousands, while their opponents were in great force. But Huan Hsüan, fearing the fate which was in store for him should he be overcome, had a light boat made fast to the side of his war-junk, so that he might escape, if necessary, at a moment's notice. The natural result was that the fighting spirit of his soldiers was utterly quenched, and when the loyalists made an attack from windward with fireships, all striving with the utmost ardour to be first in the fray, Huan Hsüan's forces were routed, had to burn all their baggage and fled for two days and nights without stopping.

Chang Yü tells a somewhat similar story of Chao Ying-Ch'i, a general of the Chin State who during a battle with the army of Ch'u in 597 B.C. had a boat kept in readiness for him on the river, wishing in case of defeat to be the first to get across.

Cowards do not count in battle; they are there but not in it.

Euripides, *Meleager* (fifth century B.C.)

---

(3) a hasty temper, which can be provoked by insults;

Tu Mu tells us that Yao Hsiang, when opposed in 357 A.D. by Huang Mei, Têng Ch'iang and others, shut himself up behind his walls and refused to fight. Têng Ch'iang said: "Our adversary is of a choleric temper and easily provoked; let us make constant sallies and break down his walls, then he will grow angry and come out. Once we can bring his force to battle, it is doomed to be our prey." This plan was acted upon, Yao Hsiang came out to fight, was lured on as far as San-yüan by the enemy's pretended flight, and finally attacked and slain.

---

(4) a delicacy of honour which is sensitive to shame;

This need not be taken to mean that a sense of honour is really a defect in a general. What Sun Tzu condemns is rather an exaggerated sensitiveness to slanderous reports, the thin-skinned man who is stung by opprobrium, however undeserved. Mei Yao-ch'ên truly observes, though somewhat paradoxically: "The seeker after glory should be careless of public opinion."

----

(5) over-solicitude for his men, which exposes him to worry and trouble.

Here again, Sun Tzu does not mean that the general is to be careless of the welfare of his troops. All he wishes to emphasise is the danger of sacrificing any important military advantage to the immediate comfort of his men. This is a shortsighted policy, because in the long run the troops will suffer more from the defeat, or, at best, the prolongation of the war, which will be the consequence. A mistaken feeling of pity will often induce a general to relieve a beleaguered city, or to reinforce a hard-pressed detachment, contrary to his military instincts.

It is now generally admitted that [Britain's] repeated efforts to relieve Ladysmith in the South African War were so many strategical blunders which defeated their own purpose. And in the end, relief came through the very man who started out with the distinct resolve no longer to subordinate the interests of the whole to sentiment in favour of a part. An old soldier of one of [the] generals who failed most conspicuously in this war, tried once, I remember, to defend him to me on the ground that he was always "so good to his men." By this plea, had he but known it, he was only condemning him out of Sun Tzu's mouth.

> A prince who gets a reputation for good nature in the first year of his reign, is laughed at in the second.
> Napoleon I, letter to the King of Holland (1807)

----

13. These are the five besetting sins of a general, ruinous to the conduct of war.

14. When an army is overthrown and its leader slain, the cause will surely be found among these five dangerous faults. Let them be a subject of meditation.

行軍篇

IX.

THE ARMY ON THE MARCH

———⌇———

The conduct of war . . . consists in the planning and conduct of fighting. . . . [Fighting] consists of a greater or lesser number of single acts, each complete in itself, which . . . are called "engagements." . . . This gives rise to the completely different activity of planning and executing these engagements themselves, and of co-ordinating each of them with the others in order to further the object of the war. One has been called tactics, and the other, strategy."

    Carl von Clausewitz, *On War* (1832)

✦ ✦ ✦

1. Sun Tzu said: We come now to the question of encamping the army, and observing signs of the enemy. Pass quickly over mountains, and keep in the neighbourhood of valleys.

The idea is, not to linger among barren uplands, but to keep close to supplies of water and grass. . . . [Compare this to Wu Tzu, who says:] "Abide not in natural ovens"; *i.e.*, "the openings of large valleys." Chang Yü tells the following anecdote: "Wu-tu Ch'iang was a robber captain in the time of the Later Han, and Ma Yüan was sent to exterminate his gang. Ch'iang having found a refuge in the hills, Ma Yüan made no attempt to force a battle, but seized all the favourable positions commanding supplies of water and forage. Ch'iang was soon in such a desperate plight for want of provisions that he was forced to make a total

surrender. He did not know the advantage of keeping in the neighbourhood of valleys."

———————

2. Camp in high places,

Not on high hills, but on knolls or hillocks elevated above the surrounding country.

———————

facing the sun.

Tu Mu takes this to mean "facing south," and Ch'ên Hao "facing east."

———————

Do not climb heights in order to fight. So much for mountain
warfare.

3. After crossing a river, you should get far away from it.

"In order to tempt the enemy to cross after you," according to Ts'ao
Kung, and also, says Chang Yü, "in order not to be impeded in your
evolutions."

———————

4. When an invading force crosses a river in its onward
march, do not advance to meet it in mid-stream. It will be best
to let half the army get across, and then deliver your attack.

Li Ch'üan alludes to the great victory won by Han Hsin over Lung Chü
at the Wei River . . . : "The two armies were drawn up on opposite sides
of the river. In the night, Han Hsin ordered his men to take some ten
thousand sacks filled with sand and construct a dam a little higher up.
Then, leading half his army across, he attacked Lung Chü; but after a
time, pretending to have failed in his attempt, he hastily withdrew to
the other bank. "Lung Chü was much elated by this unlooked-for success, and exclaiming, "I felt sure that Han Hsin was really a coward!"
he pursued him and began crossing the river in his turn. Han Hsin now
sent a party to cut open the sandbags, thus releasing a great volume of
water, which swept down and prevented the greater portion of Lung
Chü's army from getting across. He then turned upon the force which
had been cut off, and annihilated it, Lung Chü himself being amongst
the slain. The rest of the army, on the further bank, also scattered and
fled in all directions."

———————

5. If you are anxious to fight, you should not go to meet the invader near a river which he has to cross.

6. Moor your craft higher up than the enemy, and facing the sun.

Chang Yü has the note: "Said either of troops marshalled on the river-bank, or of boats anchored in the stream itself; in either case it is essential to be higher than the enemy and facing the sun."

Do not move up-stream to meet the enemy.

Tu Mu says: "As water flows downwards, we must not pitch our camp on the lower reaches of a river, for fear the enemy should open the sluices and sweep us away in a flood. . . . Chu-ko Wu-hou has remarked that 'in river warfare, we must not advance against the stream,' which is as much as to say that our fleet must not be anchored below that of the enemy, for then they would be able to take advantage of the current and make short work of us." There is also the danger, noted by other commentators, that the enemy may throw poison on the water to be carried down to us.

So much for river warfare.

7. In crossing salt-marshes, your sole concern should be to get over them quickly, without any delay.

Because of the lack of fresh water, the poor quality of the herbage, and last but not least, because they are low, flat, and exposed to attack.

8. If forced to fight in a salt-marsh, you should have water and grass near you, and get your back to a clump of trees.

Li Ch'üan remarks that the ground is less likely to be treacherous where there are trees, while Tu Yu says that they will serve to protect the rear.

So much for operations in salt-marshes.

9. In dry, level country, take up an easily accessible position

Tu Mu explains it as "ground that is smooth and firm," and therefore adapted for cavalry; Chang Yü as "level ground, free from depressions and hollows." He adds later on that although Sun Tzu is discussing flat country, there will nevertheless be slight elevations and hillocks.

---

with rising ground to your right and on your rear,

Tu Mu quotes T'ai Kung as saying: "An army should have a stream or a marsh on its left, and a hill or tumulus on its right."

---

so that the danger may be in front, and safety lie behind. So much for campaigning in flat country.

10. These are the four useful branches of military knowledge

Those, namely, concerned with (1) mountains, (2) rivers, (3) marshes, and (4) plains. Compare Napoleon's "Military Maxims," no. 1.

---

which enabled the Yellow Emperor to vanquish four several sovereigns.

Ts'ao Kung's explanation is, that the Yellow Emperor was the first to institute the feudal system of vassal princes, each of whom (to the number of four) originally bore the title of Emperor. Li Ch'üan tells us that the art of war originated under Huang Ti, who received it from his Minister Fêng Hou.

---

11. All armies prefer high ground to low,

"High ground," says Mei Yao-ch'ên, "is not only more agreeable and salubrious, but more convenient from a military point of view; low ground is not only damp and unhealthy, but also disadvantageous for fighting."

---

and sunny places to dark.

12. If you are careful of your men,

Ts'ao Kung says: "Make for fresh water and pasture, where you can turn out your animals to graze." And the other commentators follow him. . . . [My reading] has reference to the health of the troops. It is the title for Chuang Tzu's third chapter, where it denotes moral rather than physical well-being.

---

and camp on hard ground,

Dry and solid, as opposed to damp and marshy, ground. This is to be found as a rule in high places.

———————

the army will be free from disease of every kind,

Chang Yü says: "The dryness of the climate will prevent the outbreak of illness."

———————

and this will spell victory.

13. When you come to a hill or a bank, occupy the sunny side, with the slope on your right rear. Thus you will at once act for the benefit of your soldiers and utilise the natural advantages of the ground.

14. When, in consequence of heavy rains up-country, a river which you wish to ford is swollen and flecked with foam, you must wait until it subsides.

15. Country in which there are precipitous cliffs with torrents running between, deep natural hollows,

Explained [by Mei Yao-ch'ên] as "places enclosed on every side by steep banks, with pools of water at the bottom."

———————

confined places,

"Natural pens or prisons," explained as "places surrounded by precipices on three sides—easy to get into, but hard to get out of."

———————

tangled thickets,

"Places covered with such dense undergrowth that spears cannot be used."

———————

quagmires

"Low-lying places, so heavy with mud as to be impassable for chariots and horsemen."

———————

and crevasses,

[According to Mei Yao-ch'ên] "a narrow difficult way between beetling cliffs," but Ts'ao Kung [denotes] something on a much smaller scale. Tu Mu's note is "ground covered with trees and rocks, and intersected by numerous ravines and pitfalls." This is very vague, but Chia Lin explains it clearly enough as a defile or narrow pass, and Chang Yü takes much the same view.

–––––––––

should be left with all possible speed and not approached.

16. While we keep away from such places, we should get the enemy to approach them; while we face them, we should let the enemy have them on his rear.

17. If in the neighbourhood of your camp there should be any hilly country, ponds surrounded by aquatic grass, hollow basins filled with reeds, or woods with thick undergrowth, they must be carefully routed out and searched; for these are places where men in ambush or insidious spies are likely to be lurking.

Chang Yü has the note: "We must also be on our guard against traitors who may lie in close covert, secretly spying out our weaknesses and overhearing our instructions."

–––––––––

18. When the enemy is close at hand and remains quiet, he is relying on the natural strength of his position.

Here begin Sun Tzu's remarks on the reading of signs, much of which is so good that it could almost be included in a modern manual like Gen. Baden-Powell's "Aids to Scouting" [the reference is to Gen. R. S. S. Baden-Powell's military manual *Aids to Scouting for NCOs and Men* (1899)].

–––––––––

19. When he keeps aloof and tries to provoke a battle, he is anxious for the other side to advance.

Probably because we are in a strong position from which he wishes to dislodge us. "If he came close up to us," says Tu Mu, "and tried to force a battle, he would seem to despise us, and there would be less probability of our responding to the challenge."

–––––––––

20. If his place of encampment is easy of access, he is tendering a bait.

21. Movement amongst the trees of a forest shows that the enemy is advancing.

Ts'ao Kung explains this as "felling trees to clear a passage," and Chang Yü says: "Every army sends out scouts to climb high places and observe the enemy. If a scout sees that the trees of a forest are moving and shaking, he may know that they are being cut down to clear a passage for the enemy's march."

The appearance of a number of screens in the midst of thick grass means that the enemy wants to make us suspicious.

Tu Yu's explanation, borrowed from Ts'ao Kung, is as follows: "The presence of a number of screens or sheds in the midst of thick vegetation is a sure sign that the enemy has fled and, fearing pursuit, has constructed these hiding-places in order to make us suspect an ambush." It appears that these "screens" were hastily knotted together out of any long grass which the retreating army happened to come across.

22. The rising of birds in their flight is the sign of an ambuscade.

Chang Yü's explanation is doubtless right: "When birds that are flying along in a straight line suddenly shoot upwards, it means that soldiers are in ambush at the spot beneath."

Startled beasts indicate that a sudden attack is coming.

23. When there is dust rising in a high column, it is the sign of chariots advancing; when the dust is low, but spread over a wide area, it betokens the approach of infantry.

The commentators explain the phenomenon by saying that horses and chariots, being heavier than men, raise more dust, and also follow one another in the same wheel-track, whereas foot-soldiers would be marching in ranks, many abreast. According to Chang Yü, "every army on the march must have scouts some way in advance, who on sighting dust raised by the enemy, will gallop back and report it to the commander-in-chief." [As] Gen. Baden-Powell [writes]: "As you move along, say, in a hostile country, your eyes should be looking afar for the enemy or any signs of him: figures, dust rising, birds getting up, glitter of arms, etc." [*Aids to Scouting*].

When it branches out in different directions, it shows that parties have been sent to collect firewood. A few clouds of dust moving to and fro signify that the army is encamping.

Chang Yü says: "In apportioning the defences for a cantonment, light horse will be sent out to survey the position and ascertain the weak and strong points all along its circumference. Hence the small quantity of dust and its motion."

---

24. Humble words and increased preparations are signs that the enemy is about to advance.

"As though they stood in great fear of us," says Tu Mu. "Their object is to make us contemptuous and careless, after which they will attack us."

Chang Yü alludes to the story of T'ien Tan of the Ch'i State, who, in 279 B.C. was hard-pressed in his defence of Chi-mo against the Yen forces, led by Ch'i Chieh. In . . . the *Shih Chi* we read: "T'ien Tan openly said, 'My only fear is that the Yen army may cut off the noses of their Ch'i prisoners and place them in the front rank to fight against us; that would be the undoing of our city.' The other side being informed of this speech, at once acted on the suggestion; but those within the city were enraged at seeing their fellow-countrymen thus mutilated, and fearing only lest they should fall into the enemy's hands, were nerved to defend themselves more obstinately than ever.

"Once again T'ien Tan sent back converted spies who reported these words to the enemy: 'What I dread most is that the men of Yen may dig up the ancestral tombs outside the town, and by inflicting this indignity on our forefathers cause us to become faint-hearted.' Forthwith the besiegers dug up all the graves and burned the corpses lying in them. And the inhabitants of Chi-mo, witnessing the outrage from the city walls, wept passionately and were all impatient to go out and fight, their fury being increased tenfold. T'ien Tan knew then that his soldiers were ready for any enterprise. But instead of a sword, he himself took a mattock in his hands, and ordered others to be distributed amongst his best warriors, while the ranks were filled up with their wives and concubines.

He then served out all the remaining rations and bade his men eat their fill. The regular soldiers were told to keep out of sight, and the walls were manned with the old and weaker men and with women.

"This done, envoys were despatched to the enemy's camp to arrange the terms of surrender, whereupon the Yen army began shouting for joy. T'ien Tan also collected 20,000 ounces of silver from the people, and got the wealthy citizens of Chi-mo to send it to the Yen general with the prayer that, when the town capitulated, he would not allow their homes to be plundered or their women to be maltreated. Ch'i Chieh, in high good humour, granted their prayer; but his army now became increasingly slack and careless.

"Meanwhile, T'ien Tan got together a thousand oxen, decked them with pieces of red silk, painted their bodies, dragon-like, with coloured stripes, and fastened sharp blades on their horns and well-greased rushes on their tails. When the night came on, he lighted the ends of the rushes, and drove the oxen through a number of holes which he had pierced in the walls, backing them up with a force of 5000 picked warriors. The animals, maddened with pain, dashed furiously into the enemy's camp where they caused the utmost confusion and dismay; for their tails acted as torches, showing up the hideous pattern on their bodies, and the weapons on their horns killed or wounded any with whom they came into contact.

"In the meantime, the band of 5000 had crept up with gags in their mouths, and now threw themselves on the enemy. At the same moment a frightful din arose in the city itself, all those that remained behind making as much noise as possible by banging drums and hammering on bronze vessels, until heaven and earth were convulsed by the uproar. Terror-stricken, the Yen army fled in disorder, hotly pursued by the men of Ch'i, who succeeded in slaying their general Ch'i Chieh . . . The result of the battle was the ultimate recovery of some seventy cities which had belonged to the Ch'i State."

Violent language and driving forward as if to the attack are signs that he will retreat.

25. When the light chariots come out first and take up a position on the wings, it is a sign that the enemy is forming for battle.

26. Peace proposals unaccompanied by a sworn covenant indicate a plot.

27. When there is much running about

Every man hastening to his proper place under his own regimental banner.

---

and the soldiers fall into rank, it means that the critical moment has come.

28. When some are seen advancing and some retreating, it is a lure.

29. When the soldiers stand leaning on their spears, they are faint from want of food.

30. If those who are sent to draw water begin by drinking themselves, the army is suffering from thirst.

As Tu Mu remarks: "One may know the condition of a whole army from the behaviour of a single man."

---

31. If the enemy sees an advantage to be gained and makes no effort to secure it, the soldiers are exhausted.

32. If birds gather on any spot, it is unoccupied.

A useful fact to bear in mind when, for instance, as Ch'ên Hao says, the enemy has secretly abandoned his camp.

Clamour by night betokens nervousness.

Owing to false alarms; or, as Tu Mu explains it: "Fear makes men restless; so they fall to shouting at night in order to keep up their courage."

---

33. If there is disturbance in the camp, the general's authority is weak. If the banners and flags are shifted about, sedition is afoot. If the officers are angry, it means that the men are weary.

And therefore, as Capt. Calthrop says, slow to obey. Tu Mu understands the sentence differently: "If all the officers of an army are angry with their general, it means that they are broken with fatigue" [owing to the exertions which he has demanded from them].

---

34. When an army feeds its horses with grain and kills its cattle for food,

In the ordinary course of things, the men would be fed on grain and the horses chiefly on grass.

———

and when the men do not hang their cooking-pots over the camp-fires, showing that they will not return to their tents, you may know that they are determined to fight to the death.

I may quote here the illustrative passage from the *Hou Han Shu*, ... in abbreviated form ... : "The rebel Wang Kuo of Liang was besieging the town of Ch'ên-ts'ang. Huang-fu Sung, who was in supreme command, and Tung Cho were sent out against him. The latter pressed for hasty measures, but Sung turned a deaf ear to his counsel. At last the rebels were utterly worn out, and began to throw down their weapons of their own accord. Sung was now for advancing to the attack, but Cho said: 'It is a principle of war not to pursue desperate men and not to press a retreating host.' Sung answered: 'That does not apply here. What I am about to attack is a jaded army, not a retreating host; with disciplined troops I am falling on a disorganised multitude, not a band of desperate men.' Thereupon he advanced to the attack unsupported by his colleague, and routed the enemy, Wang Kuo being slain."

———

35. The sight of men whispering together in small knots or speaking in subdued tones points to disaffection amongst the rank and file.

The musket made the infantryman, and the infantryman made the democrat.
        Gen. J. F. C. Fuller, *The Conduct of War* (1961)

———

36. Too frequent rewards signify that the enemy is at the end of his resources;

Because, when an army is hard pressed, as Tu Mu says, there is always a fear of mutiny, and lavish rewards are given to keep the men in good temper.

———

too many punishments betray a condition of dire distress.

Because in such case discipline becomes relaxed, and unwonted severity is necessary to keep the men to their duty.

———

37. To begin by bluster, but afterwards to take fright at the enemy's numbers, shows a supreme lack of intelligence.

Another possible meaning, set forth by Tu Yu, Chia Lin, Mei Yao-ch'ên and Wang Hsi, is: "The general who is first tyrannical towards his men, and then in terror lest they should mutiny, etc." This would connect the sentence with what went before about rewards and punishments.

---

38. When envoys are sent with compliments in their mouths, it is a sign that the enemy wishes for a truce.

Tu Mu says: "If the enemy opens friendly relations by sending hostages, it is a sign that they are anxious for an armistice, either because their strength is exhausted or for some other reason."

---

39. If the enemy's troops march up angrily and remain facing ours for a long time without either joining battle or taking themselves off again, the situation is one that demands great vigilance and circumspection.

As Ts'ao Kung points out, a manœuvre of this sort may be only a *ruse* to gain time for an unexpected flank attack or the laying of an ambush.

---

40. If our troops are no more in number than the enemy, that is amply sufficient; it only means that no direct attack can be made.

Literally [with reference to the latter phrase], "no martial advance." That is to say, *chéng* tactics and frontal attacks must be eschewed, and stratagem resorted to instead.

What we can do is simply to concentrate all our available strength, keep a close watch on the enemy, and obtain reinforcements.

This is an obscure sentence, and none of the commentators succeed in squeezing very good sense out of it. . . . I follow Li Ch'üan, who appears to offer the simplest explanation: "Only the side that gets more men will win." . . . Chang Yü [expounds the] meaning to us in language which is lucidity itself: "When the numbers are even, and no favourable opening presents itself, although we may not be strong enough to deliver a sustained attack, we can find additional recruits amongst our sutlers and camp-followers, and then, concentrating our forces and keeping a close watch on the enemy, contrive to snatch the victory. But we must avoid borrowing foreign soldiers to help us."

He then quotes from Wei Liao Tzu . . . : "The nominal strength of mercenary troops may be 100,000, but their real value will be not more than half that figure." [Chang Yü's] interpretation means "to get recruits," not from the outside, but from the tag-rag and bobtail which follows in the wake of a large army. This does not sound a very soldierly suggestion, and I feel convinced that it is not what Sun Tzu meant.

---

41. He who exercises no forethought but makes light of his opponents is sure to be captured by them.

Ch'ên Hao [says, quoting from the *Tso Chuan*]: "If bees and scorpions carry poison, how much more will a hostile state! Even a puny opponent, then, should not be treated with contempt."

---

42. If soldiers are punished before they have grown attached to you, they will not prove submissive; and, unless submissive, they will be practically useless. If, when the soldiers have become attached to you, punishments are not enforced, they will still be useless.

43. Therefore soldiers must be treated in the first instance with humanity, but kept under control by means of iron discipline.

Yen Tzu (B.C. 493) said of Ssu-ma Jang-chü, "His civil virtues endeared him to the people; his martial prowess kept his enemies in awe." [Wu Tzu says]: "The ideal commander unites culture with a warlike temper; the profession of arms requires a combination of hardness and tenderness."

Is it better to be loved than feared, or the reverse? The answer is that it is desirable to be both, but because it is difficult to join them together, it is much safer for a prince to be feared than loved, if he is to fall in one of the two.

Niccolò Machiavelli, *The Prince* (1532)

This is a certain road to victory.

44. If in training soldiers commands are habitually enforced, the army will be well-disciplined; if not, its discipline will be bad.

45. If a general shows confidence in his men but always insists on his orders being obeyed,

Tu Mu . . . says: "A general ought in time of peace to show kindly confidence in his men and also make his authority respected, so that when they come to face the enemy, orders may be executed and discipline maintained, because they all trust and look up to him."

———————

the gain will be mutual.

Chang Yü says: "The general has confidence in the men under his command, and the men are docile, having confidence in him. Thus the gain is mutual." He quotes a pregnant sentence from Wei Liao Tzu . . . : "The art of giving orders is not to try to rectify minor blunders and not to be swayed by petty doubts." Vacillation and fussiness are the surest means of sapping the confidence of an army.

———————

地形篇

X.

TERRAIN

———— ✑ ————

Living high up on a cliff monastery, surrounded by hostile armies in command of all the roads, Mao was compelled to revise all his thinking on revolutionary tactics and strategy. . . . [H]e had commanded small guerrilla battles where his own troops possessed swift mobility . . . [and] suffered dreadful losses. His next step was to acquire the good will of the villagers on the plains, the second was to employ them as his intelligence staff, and the third was to invite the provincial armies to attack, so that he could replenish his diminishing supply of ammunition. He said later that there was not a single machine gun among his troops at the beginning. . . . [They] were successful because they knew their terrain better, because they were trained for guerrilla warfare, and because they observed all the classic tenets of guerrilla warfare without ever forgetting their main objective: loot, elbowroom, secure footholds.

Robert Payne, *Mao Tse-tung* (1969)

◆ ◆ ◆

Only about a third of the chapter, comprising paragraphs 1–13, deals with ground. . . . The "six calamities" are discussed in paragraphs 14–20, and the rest of the chapter is again a mere string of desultory remarks, though not less interesting, perhaps, on that account.

————————

1. Sun Tzu said: We may distinguish six kinds of terrain, to wit: (1) Accessible ground;

Mei Yao-ch'ên says: "Plentifully provided with roads and means of communication."

_____

(2) entangling ground;

Mei Yao-ch'ên says: "Net-like country, venturing into which you become entangled."

_____

(3) temporising ground; (4) narrow passes; (5) precipitous heights;

The root [ideas are] narrowness [and] steepness

_____

(6) positions at a great distance from the enemy.

It is hardly necessary to point out the faultiness of this classification.

_____

2. Ground which can be freely traversed by both sides is called *accessible*.

Generally speaking, "level country" is meant.

_____

3. With regard to ground of this nature, be before the enemy in occupying the raised and sunny spots, and carefully guard your line of supplies.

The general meaning is doubtless, as Tu Yu says, "not to allow the enemy to cut your communications." Tu Mu, who was not a soldier and can hardly have had any practical experience of fighting, goes more into detail and speaks of protecting the line of communications by a wall, or enclosing it by embankments on either side! In view of Napoleon's dictum, "the secret of war lies in the communications" [*Pensées de Napoléon Ier*, no. 47], we could wish that Sun Tzu had done more than skirt the edge of this important subject here and in chapter I, paragraph 10, and chapter VII, paragraph 11.

Col. Henderson says: "The line of supply may be said to be as vital to the existence of an army as the heart to the life of a human being. Just as the duelist who finds his adversary's point menacing him with certain death, and his own guard astray, is compelled to conform to his adversary's movements, and to content himself with warding off his thrusts, so the commander whose communications are suddenly threatened finds himself in a false position, and he will be fortunate if he has not to change all his plans, to split up his force into more or less isolated detachments, and to fight with inferior numbers on ground which he has not had time to prepare, and where defeat will not be an ordinary failure, but will entail the ruin or surrender of his whole army" [*The Science of War*, chapter 2].

———————

Then you will be able to fight with advantage.

4. Ground which can be abandoned but is hard to re-occupy is called *entangling*.

5. From a position of this sort, if the enemy is unprepared, you may sally forth and defeat him. But if the enemy is prepared for your coming, and you fail to defeat him, then, return being impossible, disaster will ensue.

6. When the position is such that neither side will gain by making the first move, it is called *temporising* ground.

Tu Yu writes: "Each side finds it inconvenient to move, and the situation remains at a deadlock."

———————

7. In a position of this sort, even though the enemy should offer us an attractive bait,

Tu Yu says: "turning their backs on us and pretending to flee." But this is only one of the lures which might induce us to quit our position.

———————

it will be advisable not to stir forth, but rather to retreat, thus enticing the enemy in his turn; then, when part of his army has come out, we may deliver our attack with advantage.

8. With regard to *narrow passes*, if you can occupy them first, let them be strongly garrisoned and await the advent of the enemy.

Because then, as Tu Yu observes, "the initiative will lie with us, and by making sudden and unexpected attacks we shall have the enemy at our mercy."

———————

9. Should the enemy forestall you in occupying a pass, do not go after him if the pass is fully garrisoned, but only if it is weakly garrisoned.

10. With regard to *precipitous heights*, if you are beforehand with your adversary, you should occupy the raised and sunny spots, and there wait for him to come up.

Ts'ao Kung says: "The particular advantage of securing heights and defiles is that your actions cannot then be dictated by the enemy." Chang Yü tells the following anecdote of P'ei Hsing-chien (A.D. 619–682), who was sent on a punitive expedition against the Turkic tribes: "At nightfall he pitched his camp as usual, and it had already been completely fortified by wall and ditch, when suddenly he gave orders that the army should shift its quarters to a hill near by. This was highly displeasing to his officers, who protested loudly against the extra fatigue which it would entail on the men.

"P'ei Hsing-chien, however, paid no heed to their remonstrances and had the camp moved as quickly as possible. The same night, a terrific storm came on, which flooded their former place of encampment to the depth of over twelve feet. The recalcitrant officers were amazed at the sight, and owned that they had been in the wrong. 'How did you know what was going to happen?' they asked. P'ei Hsing-chien replied: 'From this time forward be content to obey orders without asking unnecessary questions.' From this it may be seen . . . that high and sunny places are advantageous not only for fighting, but also because they are immune from disastrous floods."

———————

11. If the enemy has occupied them before you, do not follow him, but retreat and try to entice him away.

The turning-point of Li Shih-min's campaign in 621 A.D. against the two rebels, Tou Chien-tê, King of Hsia, and Wang Shih-ch'ung, Prince of Chêng, was his seizure of the heights of Wu-lao, in spite of which Tou Chien-tê persisted in his attempt to relieve his ally in Lo-yang, [and] was defeated and taken prisoner.

———————

12. If you are situated at a great distance from the enemy, and the strength of the two armies is equal, it is not easy to provoke a battle,

The point of course is, that we must not think of undertaking a long and wearisome march, at the end of which "we should be exhausted and our adversary fresh and keen."

---

and fighting will be to your disadvantage.

13. These six are the principles connected with Earth.

Or perhaps, "the principles relating to ground."

The general who has attained a responsible post must be careful to study them.

Out of the foregoing six, it will be noticed that nos. 3 and 6 have really no reference to the configuration of the country, and that only 4 and 5 can be said to convey any definite geographical idea.

---

14. Now an army is exposed to six several calamities, not arising from natural causes, but from faults for which the general is responsible. These are: (1) Flight; (2) insubordination; (3) collapse; (4) ruin; (5) disorganisation; (6) rout.

15. Other conditions being equal, if one force is hurled against another ten times its size, the result will be the *flight* of the former.

See chapter III, paragraph 10. The general's fault here is that of "not calculating the enemy's strength." . . . As Li Ch'üan very justly remarks, "Given a decided advantage in position, or the help of some stratagem such as a flank attack or an ambuscade, it would be quite possible [to fight in the ratio of one to ten]."

---

16. When the common soldiers are too strong and their officers too weak, the result is *insubordination*.

Tu Mu cites the unhappy case of T'ien Pu, who was sent to Wei in 821 A.D. with orders to lead an army against Wang T'ing-ts'ou. But the whole time he was in command, his soldiers treated him with the utmost contempt, and openly flouted his authority by riding about the camp on donkeys, several thousands at a time. T'ien Pu was powerless to put a stop to this conduct, and when, after some months had passed, he made an attempt to engage the enemy, his troops turned tail and dispersed in every direction. After that, the unfortunate man committed suicide by cutting his throat.

———————

When the officers are too strong and the common soldiers too weak, the result is *collapse*.

———————

Ts'ao Kung says: "The officers are energetic and want to press on, the common soldiers are feeble and suddenly collapse." . . . Tu Mu explains it as "stumbling into a death-trap."

———————

17. When the higher officers are angry and insubordinate, and on meeting the enemy give battle on their own account from a feeling of resentment, before the commander-in-chief can tell whether or no he is in a position to fight, the result is *ruin*.

———————

Wang Hsi's note is: "This means, the general is angry without just cause, and at the same time does not appreciate the ability of his subordinate officers; thus he arouses fierce resentment and brings an avalanche of ruin upon his head." . . . My interpretation of the whole passage is that of Mei Yao-ch'ên and Chang Yü. Tu Mu gives a long extract from the *Tso Chuan*, showing how the great battle of Pi [597 B.C.] was lost for the Chin State through the contumacy of Hsien Hu and the resentful spite of Wei I and Chao Chan.

———————

18. When the general is weak and without authority; when his orders are not clear and distinct;

———————

Wei Liao Tzu says: "If the commander gives his orders with decision, the soldiers will not wait to hear them twice; if his moves are made without vacillation, the soldiers will not be in two minds about doing their duty." General Baden-Powell says, italicising the words, "The secret of getting successful work out of your trained men lies in one nutshell—in the clearness of the instructions they receive." . . . Wu Tzu [says]: "The most fatal defect in a military leader is diffidence; the worst calamities that befall an army arise from hesitation" [*Aids to Scouting*].

———————

when there are no fixed duties assigned to officers and men,

[Tu Mu puts it thus]: "Neither officers nor men have any regular routine."

---

and the ranks are formed in a slovenly haphazard manner, the result is utter *disorganisation*.

19. When a general, unable to estimate the enemy's strength, allows an inferior force to engage a larger one, or hurls a weak detachment against a powerful one, and neglects to place picked soldiers in the front rank, the result must be a *rout*.

[From Julius Caesar's first rules in "De Bello Gallico" (the Gallic Wars)]: "Whenever there is fighting to be done, the keenest spirits should be appointed to serve in the front ranks, both in order to strengthen the resolution of our own men and to demoralise the enemy."

---

20. These are six ways of courting defeat,

Ch'ên Hao makes them out to be: (1) "neglect to estimate the enemy's strength"; (2) "want of authority"; (3) "defective training"; (4) "unjustifiable anger"; (5) "non-observance of discipline"; (6) "failure to use picked men."

---

which must be carefully noted by the general who has attained a responsible post.

21. The natural formation of the country is the soldier's best ally;

Ch'ên Hao says: "The advantages of weather and season are not equal to those connected with ground."

---

but a power of estimating the adversary,

A general should always utilise, but never rely wholly on natural advantages of terrain.

---

of controlling the forces of victory,

158 THE ART OF WAR WITH COMMENTARIES

This is one of those condensed expressions which mean so much in Chinese, and so little in an English translation. What it seems to imply is complete mastery of the situation from the beginning.

---

and of shrewdly calculating difficulties, dangers and distances, constitutes the test of a great general.

As Chang Yü remarks, these are "the essentials of soldiering," ground being only a helpful accessory.

---

22. He who knows these things, and in fighting puts his knowledge into practice, will win his battles. He who knows them not, nor practises them, will surely be defeated.

23. If fighting is sure to result in victory, then you must fight, even though the ruler forbid it; if fighting will not result in victory, then you must not fight even at the ruler's bidding.

Huang Shih-kung of the Ch'in dynasty [says]: "The responsibility of setting an army in motion must devolve on the general alone; if advance and retreat are controlled from the Palace, brilliant results will hardly be achieved. Hence the god-like ruler and the enlightened monarch are content to play a humble part in furthering their country's cause [*literally*, kneel down to push the chariot wheel]." This means that "in matters lying outside the *zenana*, the decision of the military commander must be absolute." Chang Yü also quotes the saying: "Decrees of the Son of Heaven do not penetrate the walls of a camp."

---

24. The general who advances without coveting fame and retreats without fearing disgrace,

It was Wellington, I think, who said that the hardest thing of all for a soldier is to retreat.

---

whose only thought is to protect his country and do good service for his sovereign, is the jewel of the kingdom.

A noble presentment, in few words, of the Chinese "happy warrior." Such a man, says Ho Shih, "even if he had to suffer punishment, would not regret his conduct."

---

25. Regard your soldiers as your children, and they will follow you into the deepest valleys; look on them as your own beloved sons, and they will stand by you even unto death.

In this connection, Tu Mu draws for us an engaging picture of the famous general Wu Ch'i, from whose treatise on war I have frequently had occasion to quote: "He wore the same clothes and ate the same food as the meanest of his soldiers, refused to have either a horse to ride or a mat to sleep on, carried his own surplus rations wrapped in a parcel, and shared every hardship with his men.

"One of his soldiers was suffering from an abscess, and Wu Ch'i himself sucked out the virus. The soldier's mother, hearing this, began wailing and lamenting. Somebody asked her, 'Why do you cry? Your son is only a common soldier, and yet the commander-in-chief himself has sucked the poison from his sore.' The woman replied, 'Many years ago, Lord Wu performed a similar service for my husband, who never left him afterwards, and finally met his death at the hands of the enemy. And now that he has done the same for my son, he too will fall fighting I know not where.' "

Li Ch'üan mentions the Viscount of Ch'u, who invaded the small state of Hsiao during the winter. The Duke of Shên said to him, "Many of the soldiers are suffering severely from the cold." So he made a round of the whole army, comforting and encouraging the men; and straight-way they felt as if they were clothed in garments lined with floss silk.

------

26. If, however, you are indulgent, but unable to make your authority felt; kind-hearted, but unable to enforce your commands; and incapable, moreover, of quelling disorder: then your soldiers must be likened to spoilt children; they are useless for any practical purpose.

An adage states: "Injury comes out of kindness." Li Ching once said that if you could make your soldiers afraid of you, they would not be afraid of the enemy. Tu Mu recalls an instance of stern military discipline which occurred in 219 A.D., when Lü Mêng was occupying the town of Chiang-ling. He had given stringent orders to his army not to molest the inhabitants nor take anything from them by force.

Nevertheless, a certain officer serving under his banner, who happened to be a fellow-townsman, ventured to appropriate a bamboo

hat belonging to one of the people, in order to wear it over his reg-
ulation helmet as a protection against the rain. Lü Mêng considered
that the fact of his being also a native of Ju-nan should not be allowed
to palliate a clear breach of discipline, and accordingly he ordered his
summary execution, the tears rolling down his face, however, as he
did so. This act of severity filled the army with wholesome awe, and
from that time forth even articles dropped in the highway were not
picked up.

27. If we know that our own men are in a condition to attack, but are unaware that the enemy is not open to attack, we
have gone only halfway towards victory.

That is, as Ts'ao Kung says, "the issue in this case is uncertain."

28. If we know that the enemy is open to attack, but are
unaware that our own men are not in a condition to attack, we
have gone only halfway towards victory.
29. If we know that the enemy is open to attack, and also
know that our men are in a condition to attack, but are unaware
that the nature of the ground makes fighting impracticable, we
have still gone only halfway towards victory.
30. Hence the experienced soldier, once in motion, is never
bewildered; once he has broken camp, he is never at a loss.

The reason being, according to Tu Mu, that he has taken his measures
so thoroughly as to ensure victory beforehand. "He does not move recklessly," says Chang Yü, "so that when he does move, he makes no mistakes."

31. Hence the saying: If you know the enemy and know
yourself, your victory will not stand in doubt; if you know
Heaven and know Earth, you may make your victory complete.

Li Ch'üan sums up as follows: "Given a knowledge of three things—the
affairs of man, the seasons of heaven and the natural advantages of
earth—victory will invariably crown your battles."

That the four seasons have regularities is the principle of Heaven and Earth. . . . That three seasons are for coming to completion and achievement and one season [winter] is for punishment and killing is the Dao of Heaven and Earth.

> Geoffrey MacCormack, "Mythology and the Origin of Law in Early Chinese Thought" (2001)

九 地 篇

XI.
THE NINE SITUATIONS

⎯⎯⎯⎯⎯

These can include elements of the six geographical features noted in Chapter X, as well as conditions of the army itself—that is, situations as opposed to grounds.   DG

─────────

The overwhelming lesson the PLA learned from its brushes with the Americans was the need for speed: "In the Liberation War (in China), we might take days to surround a Kuomintang division, then slowly close the circle around it. With the Americans, if we took more than a few hours, they would bring up reinforcements, aircraft, artillery."

> Yu Xiu, regimental deputy political commissar, on the storming of the 8th Cavalry's positions (1950)

✦ ✦ ✦

Wang Hsi . . . says: "There are nine military situations, good and bad."

─────────

1. Sun Tzu said: The art of war recognises nine varieties of ground: (1) Dispersive ground; (2) facile ground; (3) contentious ground; (4) open ground; (5) ground of intersecting highways; (6) serious ground; (7) difficult ground; (8) hemmed-in ground; (9) desperate ground.

2. When a chieftain is fighting in his own territory, it is dispersive ground.

So called because the soldiers, being near to their homes and anxious to see their wives and children, are likely to seize the opportunity afforded by a battle and scatter in every direction. "In their advance," observes Tu Mu, "they will lack the valour of desperation, and when they retreat, they will find harbours of refuge."

---

3. When he has penetrated into hostile territory, but to no great distance, it is facile ground.

Tu Mu remarks, "When your army has crossed the border, you should burn your boats and bridges, in order to make it clear to everybody that you have no hankering after home."

---

4. Ground the possession of which imports great advantage to either side, is contentious ground.

I must apologise for using ["contentious"] in a sense not known to the dictionary, i.e., "to be contended for." . . . Ts'ao Kung says: "ground on which the few and the weak can defeat the many and the strong," such as "the neck of a pass," instanced by Li Ch'üan. Thus, Thermopylae was [contentious ground], because the possession of it, even for a few days only, meant holding the entire invading army in check and thus gaining invaluable time. [Wu Tzu writes]: "For those who have to fight in the ratio of one to ten, there is nothing better than a narrow pass."

When Lü Kuang was returning from his triumphant expedition to Turkestan in 385 A.D., and had got as far as I-ho, laden with spoils, Liang Hsi, administrator of Liang-chou, taking advantage of the death of Fu Chien, King of Ch'in, plotted against him and was for barring his way into the province. Yang Han, governor of Kao-ch'ang, counselled him, saying, "Lü Kuang is fresh from his victories in the west, and his soldiers are vigorous and mettlesome. If we oppose him in the shifting sands of the desert, we shall be no match for him, and we must therefore try a different plan. Let us hasten to occupy the defile at the mouth of the Kao-wu pass, thus cutting him off from supplies of water, and when his troops are prostrated with thirst, we can dictate our own terms without moving. Or if you think that the pass I mention is too far off we could make a stand against him at the I-wu pass, which is nearer. The cunning and resource of Tzu-fang himself would be expended in vain against the enormous strength of these two positions." Liang Hsi, refusing to act on this advice, was overwhelmed and swept away by the invader.

---

5. Ground on which each side has liberty of movement is open ground.

Ts'ao Kung [explains this as] "ground covered with a network of roads," like a chess-board. Another interpretation, suggested by Ho Shih, is "ground on which intercommunication is easy." In either case, it must evidently be "flat country," and therefore [it] "cannot be blocked."

6. Ground which forms the key to three contiguous states,

[Ts'ao Kung writes:] "Our country adjoining the enemy's and a third country conterminous with both."

so that he who occupies it first has most of the Empire at his command,

China was divided [into a loose confederacy of states] under the Chou dynasty. The belligerent who holds this dominating position can constrain most of them to become his allies.

is ground of intersecting highways.

7. When an army has penetrated into the heart of a hostile country, leaving a number of fortified cities in its rear, it is serious ground.

Wang Hsi explains the name by saying that "when an army has reached such a point, its situation is serious." Li Ch'üan instances (1) the victorious march of Yo I into the capital of Ch'i in 284 B.C., and (2) the attack on Ch'u, six years later, by the Ch'in general Po Ch'i.

8. Mountain forests, rugged steeps, marshes and fens—all country that is hard to traverse: this is difficult ground.

Chia Lin explains [steeps, marshes and fens] as ground "that has been ruined by water passing over it," and Tu Yu simply as "swampy ground." But Ch'ên Hao says [it refers particularly] to deep hollows—what Chu-ko Liang [designated] "earth-hells."

9. Ground which is reached through narrow gorges, and from which we can only retire by tortuous paths, so that a small

number of the enemy would suffice to crush a large body of our men: this is hemmed-in ground.

10. Ground on which we can only be saved from destruction by fighting without delay, is desperate ground.

As pictured by Ts'ao Kung, ... here escape is no longer possible: "A lofty mountain in front, a large river behind, advance impossible, retreat blocked." Ch'ên Hao says: "To be on 'desperate ground' is like sitting in a leaking boat or crouching in a burning house."

Tu Mu quotes from Li Ching a vivid description of the plight of an army thus entrapped: "Suppose an army is invading hostile territory without the aid of local guides:—it falls into a fatal snare and is at the enemy's mercy. A ravine on the left, a mountain on the right, a pathway so perilous that the horses have to be roped together and the chariots carried in slings, no passage open in front, retreat cut off behind, no choice but to proceed in single file. Then, before there is time to range our soldiers in order of battle, the enemy in overwhelming strength suddenly appears on the scene. Advancing, we can nowhere take a breathing-space; retreating, we have no haven of refuge. We seek a pitched battle, but in vain; yet standing on the defensive, none of us has a moment's respite.

"If we simply maintain our ground, whole days and months will crawl by; the moment we make a move, we have to sustain the enemy's attacks on front and rear. The country is wild, destitute of water and plants; the army is lacking in the necessaries of life, the horses are jaded and the men worn-out; all the resources of strength and skill unavailing, the pass so narrow that a single man defending it can check the onset of ten thousand; all means of offence in the hands of the enemy, all points of vantage already forfeited by ourselves:—in this terrible plight, even though we had the most valiant soldiers and the keenest of weapons, how could they be employed with the slightest effect?"

Students of Greek history may be reminded of the awful close to the Sicilian expedition, and the agony of the Athenians under Nicias and Demosthenes.

———

11. On dispersive ground, therefore, fight not. On facile ground, halt not. On contentious ground, attack not.

But [according to Ts'ao Kung] rather let all your energies be bent on occupying the advantageous position first. Li Ch'üan and others, however, suppose the meaning to be that the enemy has already forestalled us, so that it would be sheer madness to attack. . . .

When the King of Wu inquires what should be done in this case, Sun Tzu replies: "The rule with regard to contentious ground is that those in possession have the advantage over the other side. If a position of this kind is secured first by the enemy, beware of attacking him. Lure him away by pretending to flee—show your banners and sound your drums—make a dash for other places that he cannot afford to lose—trail brushwood and raise a dust—confound his ears and eyes—detach a body of your best troops, and place it secretly in ambuscade. Then your opponent will sally forth to the rescue."

---

12. On open ground, do not try to block the enemy's way.

Because the attempt would be futile, and would expose the blocking force itself to serious risks [this interpretation follows] that of Chang Yü. [Another interpretation] is indicated in Ts'ao Kung's brief note: "Draw closer together"—*i.e.*, see that a portion of your own army is not cut off. Wang Hsi points out that "open ground" is only another name for the "accessible ground" described in chapter X, paragraph 2, and says that the advice here given is simply a variation of "keep a sharp eye on the line of supplies," be careful that your communications are not cut.

On ground of intersecting highways, join hands with your allies.

Or perhaps, "form alliances with neighbouring states."

> No people on earth can be held, as a people, to be an enemy, for all humanity shares the common hunger for peace and fellowship and justice. No nation's security and well-being can be lastingly achieved in isolation but only in effective cooperation with fellow-nations.
>
> President Dwight David Eisenhower, "The Chance for Peace" (1953)

---

13. On serious ground, gather in plunder.

On this, Li Ch'üan has the following delicious note: "When an army penetrates far into the enemy's country, care must be taken not to alienate the people by unjust treatment. Follow the example of the Han Emperor Kao Tsu, whose march into Ch'in territory [in 207 B.C.] was marked by no violation of women or looting of valuables. Thus he won the hearts of all. In the present passage, then, I think that the true reading must be, not 'plunder,' but 'do not plunder.'" Alas, I fear that in this instance the worthy commentator's feelings outran his judgment.

Tu Mu, at least, has no such illusions. He says: "When encamped on 'serious ground,' there being no inducement as yet to advance further, and no possibility of retreat, one ought to take measures for a protracted resistance by bringing in provisions from all sides, and keep a close watch on the enemy."

In difficult ground, keep steadily on the march.

Or, in the words of chapter VIII, paragraph 2, "do not encamp."

14. On hemmed-in ground, resort to stratagem.

Ts'ao Kung says: "Try the effect of some unusual artifice"; and Tu Yu amplifies this by saying: "In such a position, some scheme must be devised which will suit the circumstances, and if we can succeed in deluding the enemy, the peril may be escaped." This is exactly what happened on the famous occasion when Hannibal was hemmed in among the mountains on the road to Casilinum, and to all appearances entrapped by the Dictator Fabius.

The stratagem which Hannibal devised to baffle his foes was remarkably like that which T'ien Tan had also employed with success exactly 62 years before. [See the note for chapter IX, paragraph 24.] When night came on, bundles of twigs were fastened to the horns of some 2000 oxen and set on fire, the terrified animals being then quickly driven along the mountain side towards the passes which were beset by the enemy. The strange spectacle of these rapidly moving lights so alarmed and discomfited the Romans that they withdrew from their position, and Hannibal's army passed safely through the defile.

On desperate ground, fight.

For, as Chia Lin remarks, "if you fight with all your might, there is a chance of life; whereas death is certain if you cling to your corner."

15. Those who were called skilful leaders of old knew how to drive a wedge between the enemy's front and rear; to prevent co-operation between his large and small divisions; to hinder the good troops from rescuing the bad, the officers from rallying their men.

16. When the enemy's men were scattered, they prevented them from concentrating; even when their forces were united, they managed to keep them in disorder.

17. When it was to their advantage, they made a forward move; when otherwise, they stopped still.

Mei Yao-ch'ên connects this with the foregoing: "Having succeeded in thus dislocating the enemy, they would push forward in order to secure any advantage to be gained; if there was no advantage to be gained, they would remain where they were."

---

18. If asked how to cope with a great host of the enemy in orderly array and on the point of marching to the attack, I should say: "Begin by seizing something which your opponent holds dear; then he will be amenable to your will."

Opinions differ as to what Sun Tzu had in mind. Ts'ao Kung thinks it is "some strategical advantage on which the enemy is depending." Tu Mu says: "The three things which an enemy is anxious to do, and on the accomplishment of which his success depends, are: (1) to capture our favourable positions; (2) to ravage our cultivated land; (3) to guard his own communications." Our object then must be to thwart his plans in these three directions and thus render him helpless.

But . . . I agree with Ch'ên Hao, who says [the text] does not refer only to strategical advantages, but is any person or thing that may happen to be of importance to the enemy. By boldly seizing the initiative in this way, you at once throw the other side on the defensive.

---

19. Rapidity is the essence of war:

According to Tu Mu, "this is a summary of leading principles in warfare," and he adds: "These are the profoundest truths of military science, and the chief business of the general."

The following anecdotes, told by Ho Shih, show the importance attached to speed by two of China's greatest generals. In 227 A.D., Mêng

Ta, governor of Hsin-ch'êng under the Wei Emperor Wên Ti, was meditating defection to the House of Shu, and had entered into correspondence with Chu-ko Liang, Prime Minister of that State. The Wei general Ssu-ma I was then military governor of Wan, and getting wind of Mêng Ta's treachery, he at once set off with an army to anticipate his revolt, having previously cajoled him by a specious message of friendly import. Ssu-ma's officers came to him and said: "If Mêng Ta has leagued himself with Wu and Shu, the matter should be thoroughly investigated before we make a move." Ssu-ma I replied: "Mêng Ta is an unprincipled man, and we ought to go and punish him at once, while he is still wavering and before he has thrown off the mask."

Then, by a series of forced marches, he brought his army under the walls of Hsin-ch'êng within the space of eight days. Now Mêng Ta had previously said in a letter to Chu-ko Liang: "Wan is 1200 *li* from here. When the news of my revolt reaches Ssu-ma I, he will at once inform his Imperial Master, but it will be a whole month before any steps can be taken, and by that time my city will be well fortified. Besides, Ssu-ma I is sure not to come himself, and the generals that will be sent against us are not worth troubling about." The next letter, however, was filled with consternation: "Though only eight days have passed since I threw off my allegiance, an army is already at the city-gates. What miraculous rapidity is this!" A fortnight later, Hsin-ch'êng had fallen and Mêng Ta had lost his head.

In 621 A.D., Li Ching was sent from K'uei-chou in Ssu-ch'uan to reduce the successful rebel Hsiao Hsien, who had set up as Emperor at the modern Ching-chou Fu in Hupeh. It was autumn, and the Yangtsze being then in flood, Hsiao Hsien never dreamt that his adversary would venture to come down through the gorges, and consequently made no preparations. But Li Ching embarked his army without loss of time, and was just about to start when the other generals implored him to postpone his departure until the river was in a less dangerous state for navigation.

Li Ching replied: "To the soldier, overwhelming speed is of paramount importance, and he must never miss opportunities. Now is the time to strike, before Hsiao Hsien even knows that we have got an army together. If we seize the present moment when the river is in flood, we shall appear before his capital with startling suddenness, like the thunder which is heard before you have time to stop your ears against it. [See note for chapter VII, paragraph 19.] This is the great principle in war. Even if he gets to know of our approach, he will have to levy his soldiers in such a hurry that they will not be fit to oppose us. Thus the full fruits of victory will be ours." All came about as he had predicted, and Hsiao Hsien was obliged to surrender, nobly stipulating that his people should be spared and he alone suffer the penalty of death.

———

take advantage of the enemy's unreadiness, make your way by unexpected routes, and attack unguarded spots.

20. The following are the principles to be observed by an invading force: The further you penetrate into a country, the greater will be the solidarity of your troops, and thus the defenders will not prevail against you.

21. Make forays in fertile country in order to supply your army with food.

22. Carefully study the well-being of your men,

[Wang Hsi says:] "Pet them, humour them, give them plenty of food and drink, and look after them generally."

———

As you know that the Credit of the Service depends not only on dealing fairly with the men Employed in it, but on their belief that they are and will be fairly dealt with.

John Paul Jones, establishing rules for naval conduct (1777)

———

and do not overtax them. Concentrate your energy and hoard your strength.

Ch'ên recalls the line of action taken in 224 B.C. by the famous general Wang Chien, whose military genius largely contributed to the success of the First Emperor. He had invaded the Ch'u State, where a universal levy was made to oppose him. But, being doubtful of the temper of his troops, he declined all invitations to fight and remained strictly on the defensive. In vain did the Ch'u general try to force a battle: day after day Wang Chien kept inside his walls and would not come out, but devoted his whole time and energy to winning the affection and confidence of his men. He took care that they should be well fed, sharing his own meals with them, provided facilities for bathing, and employed every method of judicious indulgence to weld them into a loyal and homogeneous body.

After some time had elapsed, he told off certain persons to find out how the men were amusing themselves. The answer was, that they were contending with one another in putting the weight and long-jumping. When Wang Chien heard that they were engaged in these athletic pursuits, he knew that their spirits had been strung up to the required pitch and that they were now ready for fighting. By this time the Ch'u army, after repeating their challenge again and again, had marched away eastwards in disgust. The Ch'in general immediately broke up his camp and followed them, and in the battle that ensued they were routed with great slaughter. Shortly afterwards, the whole of Ch'u was conquered by Ch'in, and the king Fu-ch'u led into captivity.

Keep your army continually on the move,

In order that the enemy may never know exactly where you are.

and devise unfathomable plans.

23. Throw your soldiers into positions whence there is no escape, and they will prefer death to flight. If they will face death, there is nothing they may not achieve.

Chang Yü . . . quotes . . . Wei Liao Tzu: "If one man were to run amok with a sword in the market-place, and everybody else tried to get out of his way, I should not allow that this man alone had courage and that all the rest were contemptible cowards. The truth is, that a desperado and a man who sets some value on his life do not meet on even terms."

Officers and men alike will put forth their uttermost strength.

Chang Yü says: "If they are in an awkward place together, they will surely exert their united strength to get out of it."

24. Soldiers when in desperate straits lose the sense of fear. If there is no place of refuge, they will stand firm. If they are in the heart of a hostile country, they will show a stubborn front. If there is no help for it, they will fight hard.

25. Thus, without waiting to be marshalled, the soldiers will be constantly on the *qui vive*; without waiting to be asked, they will do your will;

Literally, "without asking, you will get."

without restrictions, they will be faithful; without giving orders, they can be trusted.

The whole of this paragraph, of course, has reference to "desperate ground."

---

26. Prohibit the taking of omens, and do away with superstitious doubts. Then, until death itself comes, no calamity need be feared.

The superstitious, "bound in to saucy doubts and fears," degenerate into cowards and "die many times before their deaths." Tu Mu quotes Huang Shih-kung: "'Spells and incantations should be strictly forbidden, and no officer allowed to inquire by divination into the fortunes of an army, for fear the soldiers' minds should be seriously perturbed.' The meaning is," he continues, "that if all doubts and scruples are discarded, your men will never falter in their resolution until they die."

---

27. If our soldiers are not overburdened with money, it is not because they have a distaste for riches; if their lives are not unduly long, it is not because they are disinclined to longevity.

Chang Yü has the best note on this passage, "Wealth and long life are things for which all men have a natural inclination. Hence, if they burn or fling away valuables, and sacrifice their own lives, it is not that they dislike them, but simply that they have no choice." Sun Tzu is slyly insinuating that, as soldiers are but human, it is for the general to see that temptations to shirk fighting and grow rich are not thrown in their way.

---

28. On the day they are ordered out to battle, your soldiers may weep,

The verb in Chinese is "snivel." This is taken to indicate more genuine grief than tears alone.

---

those sitting up bedewing their garments, and those lying down letting the tears run down their cheeks.

Not because they are afraid, but because, as Ts'ao Kung says, "all have embraced the firm resolution to do or die." We may remember that the heroes of the Iliad were equally childlike in showing their emotion. Chang Yü alludes to the mournful parting at the I River between Ching K'o and his friends, when the former was sent to attempt the life of the King of Ch'in (afterwards First Emperor) in 227 B.C. The tears of all flowed down like rain as he bade them farewell and uttered the following lines: "The shrill blast is blowing, Chilly the burn; Your champion is going—Not to return."

But let them once be brought to bay, and they will display the courage of a Chu or a Kuei.

[Chu] was the personal [that is, given] name of Chuan Chu, a native of the Wu State and contemporary with Sun Tzu himself, who was employed by . . . Ho Lü Wang to assassinate his sovereign Wang Liao with a dagger which he had secreted in the belly of a fish served up at a banquet. He succeeded in his attempt, but was immediately hacked to pieces by the king's bodyguard. This was in 515 B.C.

The other hero referred to, Ts'ao Kuei, performed the exploit which . . . made his name famous 166 years earlier, in 681 B.C. Lu had been thrice defeated by Ch'i, and was just about to conclude a treaty surrendering a large slice of territory, when Ts'ao Kuei suddenly seized Huan Kung, the Duke of Ch'i, as he stood on the altar steps and held a dagger against his chest. None of the Duke's retainers dared to move a muscle, and Ts'ao Kuei proceeded to demand full restitution, declaring that Lu was being unjustly treated because she was a smaller and weaker state. Huan Kung, in peril of his life, was obliged to consent, whereupon Ts'ao Kuei flung away his dagger and quietly resumed his place amid the terrified assemblage without having so much as changed colour. As was to be expected, the Duke wanted afterwards to repudiate the bargain, but his wise old counsellor Kuan Chung pointed out to him the impolicy of breaking his word, and the upshot was that this bold stroke regained for Lu the whole of what she had lost in three pitched battles.

---

29. The skilful tactician may be likened to the *shuai-jan*. Now the *shuai-jan* is a snake that is found in the Ch'ang mountains. Strike at its head, and you will be attacked by its tail; strike at its tail, and you will be attacked by its head; strike at its middle, and you will be attacked by head and tail both.

30. Asked if an army can be made to imitate the *shuai-jan*,

That is, as Mei Yao-ch'ên says, "Is it possible to make the front and rear of an army each swiftly responsive to attack on the other, just as though they were parts of a single living body?"

I should answer, Yes. For the men of Wu and the men of Yüeh are enemies; yet if they are crossing a river in the same boat and are caught by a storm, they will come to each other's assistance just as the left hand helps the right.

The meaning is: If two enemies will help each other in a time of common peril, how much more should two parts of the same army, bound together as they are by every tie of interest and fellow-feeling. Yet it is notorious that many a campaign has been ruined through lack of cooperation, especially in the case of allied armies.

31. Hence it is not enough to put one's trust in the tethering of horses, and the burying of chariot wheels in the ground.

These quaint devices to prevent one's army from running away recall the Athenian hero Sôphanes, who carried an anchor with him at the battle of Plataea, by means of which he fastened himself firmly to one spot. It is not enough, says Sun Tzu, to render flight impossible by such mechanical means. You will not succeed unless your men have tenacity and unity of purpose, and, above all, a spirit of sympathetic co-operation. This is the lesson which can be learned from the *shuai-jan*.

32. The principle on which to manage an army is to set up one standard of courage which all must reach.

Literally, "level the courage [of all] as though [it were that of] one." If the ideal army is to form a single organic whole, then it follows that the resolution and spirit of its component parts must be of the same quality, or at any rate must not fall below a certain standard. Wellington's seemingly ungrateful description of his army at Waterloo [where he won] as "the worst he had ever commanded" meant no more than that it was deficient in this important particular—unity of spirit and courage. Had he not foreseen the Belgian defections and carefully kept those troops in the background, he would most certainly have lost the day.

33. How to make the best of both strong and weak—that is a question involving the proper use of ground.

Mei Yao-ch'ên's paraphrase is: "The way to eliminate the differences of strong and weak and to make both serviceable is to utilise accidental features of the ground." Less reliable troops, if posted in strong positions, will hold out as long as better troops on more exposed terrain. The advantage of position neutralises the inferiority in stamina and courage.

Col. Henderson says: "With all respect to the text books, and to ordinary tactical teaching, I am inclined to think that the study of ground is often overlooked, and that by no means sufficient importance is attached to the selection of positions . . . and to the immense advantages that are to be derived, whether you are defending or attacking, from the proper utilisation of natural features" [*The Science of War*].

----

34. Thus the skilful general conducts his army just as though he were leading a single man, willy-nilly, by the hand.

Tu Mu says: "The simile has reference to the ease with which he does it." [The Chinese] means that he makes it impossible for his troops to do otherwise than obey.

----

35. It is the business of a general to be quiet and thus ensure secrecy; upright and just, and thus maintain order.

[The Chinese] seems to combine the meanings "noiseless" and "imperturbable," both of which attributes would of course conduce to secrecy.

----

36. He must be able to mystify his officers and men by false reports and appearances, and thus keep them in total ignorance.

Ts'ao Kung gives us one of his excellent apophthegms: "The troops must not be allowed to share your schemes in the beginning; they may only rejoice with you over the happy outcome."

"To mystify, mislead, and surprise the enemy," is one of the first principles in war, as has been frequently pointed out. But how about the other process—the mystification of one's own men? Those who may think that Sun Tzu is over-emphatic on this point would do well to read Col. Henderson's remarks on Stonewall Jackson's Valley campaign: "The infinite pains," he says, "with which Jackson sought to conceal, even from his most trusted staff officers, his movements, his intentions, and his thoughts, a commander less thorough would have pronounced useless"—etc., etc. [*Stonewall Jackson*, Vol. 1].

In the year 88 A.D., . . . , "Pan Ch'ao took the field with 25,000 men from Khotan and other Central Asian states with the object of crushing Yarkand. The King of Kutcha replied by dispatching his chief commander to succour the place with an army drawn from the kingdoms of Wên-su, Ku-mo and Wei-t'ou, totalling 50,000 men. Pan Ch'ao summoned his officers and also the King of Khotan to a council of war, and said: "Our forces are now outnumbered and unable to make head against the enemy. The best plan, then, is for us to separate and disperse, each in a different direction. The King of Khotan will march away by the easterly route, and I will then return myself towards the west. Let us wait until the evening drum has sounded and then start."

Pan Ch'ao now secretly released the prisoners whom he had taken alive, and the King of Kutcha was thus informed of his plans. Much elated by the news, the latter set off at once at the head of 10,000 horsemen to bar Pan Ch'ao's retreat in the west, while the King of Wên-su rode eastwards with 8000 horse in order to intercept the King of Khotan. As soon as Pan Ch'ao knew that the two chieftains had gone, he called his divisions together, got them well in hand, and at cock-crow hurled them against the army of Yarkand, as it lay encamped.

The barbarians, panic-stricken, fled in confusion, and were closely pursued by Pan Ch'ao. Over 5000 heads were brought back as trophies, besides immense spoils in the shape of horses and cattle and valuables of every description. Yarkand then capitulating, Kutcha and the other kingdoms drew off their respective forces. From that time forward, Pan Ch'ao's prestige completely overawed the countries of the west." In this case, we see that the Chinese general not only kept his own officers in ignorance of his real plans, but actually took the bold step of dividing his army in order to deceive the enemy.

———

37. By altering his arrangements and changing his plans, he keeps the enemy without definite knowledge.

———

Chang Yü quotes [another commentator] as saying: "The axiom, that war is based on deception, does not apply only to deception of the enemy. You must deceive even your own soldiers. Make them follow you, but without letting them know why."

———

By shifting his camp and taking circuitous routes, he prevents the enemy from anticipating his purpose.

38. At the critical moment, the leader of an army acts like one who has climbed up a height and then kicks away the ladder behind him. He carries his men deep into hostile territory before he shows his hand.

39. He burns his boats and breaks his cooking-pots; like a shepherd driving a flock of sheep, he drives his men this way and that, and none knows whither he is going.

Tu Mu says: "The army is only cognisant of orders to advance or retreat; it is ignorant of the ulterior ends of attacking and conquering."

---

40. To muster his host and bring it into danger:—this may be termed the business of the general.

Sun Tzu means that after mobilisation there should be no delay in aiming a blow at the enemy's heart. Note how he returns again and again to this point [see paragraph 23 above]. Among the warring states of ancient China, desertion was no doubt a much more present fear and serious evil than it is in the armies of to-day.

---

41. The different measures suited to the nine varieties of ground;

Chang Yü says: "One must not be hide-bound in interpreting the rules for the nine varieties of ground."

---

the expediency of aggressive or defensive tactics; and the fundamental laws of human nature: these are things that must most certainly be studied.

42. When invading hostile territory, the general principle is, that penetrating deeply brings cohesion; penetrating but a short way means dispersion.

43. When you leave your own country behind, and take your army across neighbouring territory, you find yourself on critical ground.

This "ground" is cursorily mentioned in chapter VIII, paragraph 2, but it does not figure among the nine situations of this chapter or the six kinds of terrain in chapter X. One's first impulse would be to translate it [as] "distant ground" (... in the sense of "distant lands"), but this ... is precisely what is not meant here. Mei Yao-ch'ên says it is "a position not far enough advanced to be called 'facile,' and not near enough to home to be called 'dispersive,' but something between the two."

That, of course, does not explain the name, which seems to imply that the general has severed his communications and temporarily cut himself off from his base. Thus, Wang Hsi says: "It is ground separated from home by an interjacent state, whose territory we have had to cross in order to reach it. Hence it is incumbent on us to settle our business there quickly." He adds that this position is of rare occurrence, which is the reason why it is not included among the six kinds of terrain.

When there are means of communication on all four sides, the ground is one of intersecting highways.

44. When you penetrate deeply into a country, it is serious ground. When you penetrate but a little way, it is facile ground.

45. When you have the enemy's strongholds on your rear, and narrow passes in front, it is hemmed-in ground. When there is no place of refuge at all, it is desperate ground.

46. Therefore, on dispersive ground, I would inspire my men with unity of purpose.

This end, according to Tu Mu, is best attained by remaining on the defensive, and avoiding battle.

On facile ground, I would see that there is close connection between all parts of my army.

As Tu Mu says, the object is to guard against two possible contingencies: "(1) the desertion of our own troops; (2) a sudden attack on the part of the enemy." Mei Yao-ch'ên says: "On the march, the regiments should be in close touch; in an encampment, there should be continuity between the fortifications."

---

47. On contentious ground, I would hurry up my rear.

This is Ts'ao Kung's interpretation. Chang Yü adopts it, saying: "We must quickly bring up our rear, so that head and tail may both reach the goal." That is, they must not be allowed to straggle up a long way apart. Mei Yao-ch'ên offers another equally plausible explanation: "Supposing the enemy has not yet reached the coveted position, and we are behind him, we should advance with all speed in order to dispute its possession." . . .

Ch'ên Hao, on the other hand, assuming that the enemy has had time [to] select his own ground, quotes [Sun Tzu's admonition] against coming exhausted to the attack. His own idea of the situation is rather vaguely expressed: "If there is a favourable position lying in front of you, detach a picked body of troops to occupy it; then if the enemy, relying on their numbers, come up to make a fight for it, *you may fall quickly on their rear* with your main body, and victory will be assured." It was thus, he adds, that Chao Shê beat the army of Ch'in.

---

48. On open ground, I would keep a vigilant eye on my defences.

As Wang Hsi says, "fearing a surprise attack."

On ground of intersecting highways, I would consolidate my alliances.

49. On serious ground, I would try to ensure a continuous stream of supplies.

The commentators take this as referring to forage and plunder, not, as one might expect, to an unbroken communication with a home base.

On difficult ground, I would keep pushing on along the road.

[Ts'ao Kung puts it thus:] "Pass away from it in all haste."

---

50. On hemmed-in ground, I would block any way of retreat.

[Mêng Shih says:] "To make it seem that I mean to defend the position, whereas my real intention is to burst suddenly through the enemy's lines." [Mei Yao-ch'ên says:] "In order to make my soldiers fight with desperation." [Wang Hsi says:] "Fearing lest my men be tempted to run away." Tu Mu points out that this [injunction] is the converse of chapter VII, paragraph 36, where it is the enemy who is surrounded.

In 532 A.D., Kao Huan, afterwards Emperor and canonised as Shên-wu, was surrounded by a great army under Êrh-chu Chao and others. His own force was comparatively small, consisting only of 2000 horse and something under 30,000 foot. The lines of investment had not been drawn very closely together, gaps being left at certain points. But Kao Huan, instead of trying to escape, actually made a shift to block all the remaining outlets himself by driving into them a number of oxen and donkeys roped together. As soon as his officers and men saw that there was nothing for it but to conquer or die, their spirits rose to an extraordinary pitch of exaltation, and they charged with such desperate ferocity that the opposing ranks broke and crumbled under their onslaught.

On desperate ground, I would proclaim to my soldiers the hopelessness of saving their lives.

Tu Yu says: "Burn your baggage and impedimenta, throw away your stores and provisions, choke up the wells, destroy your cooking-stoves, and make it plain to your men that they cannot survive, but must fight to the death." Mei Yao-ch'ên says epigrammatically: "The only chance of life lies in giving up all hope of it." This concludes what Sun Tzu has to say about "grounds" and the "variations" responding to them.

Reviewing the passages which bear on this important subject, we cannot fail to be struck by the desultory and unmethodical fashion in which it is treated. Sun Tzu begins abruptly in chapter VIII, paragraph 2, to enumerate "variations" before touching on "grounds" at all, but only mentions five, namely nos. 5, 7, 8 and 9 of the subsequent list, and one that is not included in it. A few varieties of ground are dealt with in the earlier portion of chapter IX, and then chapter X sets forth six new grounds, with six variations of plan to match. None of these is mentioned again [until] at last, in chapter XI, we come to the Nine Grounds *par excellence*, immediately followed by the variations. . . .

Though it is impossible to account for the present state of Sun Tzu's text, a few suggestive facts may be brought into prominence: (1) chapter VIII, according to the title, should deal with nine variations, whereas only five appear. (2) It is an abnormally short chapter. (3) Chapter XI is entitled The Nine Grounds. Several of these are defined twice over, besides which there are two distinct lists of the corresponding variations. (4) The length of the chapter is disproportionate, being double that of any other except IX. I do not propose to draw any inferences from these facts, beyond the general conclusion that Sun Tzu's work cannot have come down to us in the shape in which it left his hands: chapter VIII is obviously defective and probably out of place, while XI seems to contain matter that has either been added by a later hand or ought to appear elsewhere.

---

51. For it is the soldier's disposition to offer an obstinate resistance when surrounded, to fight hard when he cannot help himself, and to obey promptly when he has fallen into danger.

[Chang Yü] alludes to the conduct of Pan Ch'ao's devoted followers in 73 A.D.: "When Pan Ch'ao arrived at Shan-shan, Kuang, the King of the country, received him at first with great politeness and respect; but shortly afterwards his behaviour underwent a sudden change, and he became remiss and negligent. Pan Ch'ao spoke about this to the officers of his suite: 'Have you not noticed,' he said, 'that Kuang's polite intentions are on the wane? This must signify that envoys have come from the Northern barbarians, and that consequently he is in a state of indecision, not knowing with which side to throw in his lot. That surely is the reason. The truly wise man, we are told, can perceive things before they have come to pass; how much more, then, those that are already manifest!' Thereupon he called one of the natives who had been assigned to his service, and set a trap for him, saying: 'Where are those envoys from the Hsiung-nu who arrived some days ago?'

"The man was so taken aback that between surprise and fear he presently blurted out the whole truth. Pan Ch'ao, keeping his informant carefully under lock and key, then summoned a general gathering of his officers, thirty-six in all, and began drinking with them. When the wine had mounted into their heads a little, he tried to rouse their spirit still further by addressing them thus: 'Gentlemen, here we are in the heart of an isolated region, anxious to achieve riches and honour by some great exploit. Now it happens that an ambassador from the Hsiung-nu arrived in this kingdom only a few days ago, and the result is that the respectful courtesy extended towards us by our royal host has disappeared. Should this envoy prevail upon him to seize our party and hand us over to the Hsiung-nu, our bones will become food for the wolves of the desert. What are we to do?' With one accord, the officers replied, '*Standing as we do in peril of our lives, we will follow our commander through life and death.*'" For the sequel of this adventure, see chapter XII, paragraph 1, note.

---

52. We cannot enter into alliance with neighbouring princes until we are acquainted with their designs. We are not fit to lead an army on the march unless we are familiar with the face of the country—its mountains and forests, its pitfalls and precipices, its marshes and swamps. We shall be unable to turn natural advantages to account unless we make use of local guides.

These sentences are repeated from chapter VII, paragraphs 12–14—in order to emphasise their importance, the commentators seem to think. I prefer to regard them as interpolated here in order to form an antecedent to the following words. With regard to local guides, Sun Tzu might have added that there is always the risk of going wrong, either through their treachery or some misunderstanding . . . : Hannibal, we are told, ordered a guide to lead him into the neighbourhood of Casinum, where there was an important pass to be occupied; but his Carthaginian accent, unsuited to the pronunciation of Latin names, caused the guide to understand Casilinum instead of Casinum, and turning from his proper route, he took the army in that direction, the mistake not being discovered until they had almost arrived.

This mistake almost cost Hannibal his army: The troops were hemmed in by the mountains on either side of the route to Casilinum. The Roman commander, Fabius, figured he had Hannibal trapped. But in one of military history's greatest ruses, Hannibal, in a tactic similar to what T'ien Tan had used in China some sixty years earlier, took advantage of the cover of night, disguised cattle with fire to surprise and terrify his enemy, and escaped. See the note for chapter IX, paragraph 24.   DG

53. To be ignorant of any one of the following four or five principles does not befit a warlike prince.

"One who rules by force," was a term specially used for those princes who established their hegemony over other feudal states. The famous "warlike princes" of the 7th century B.C. were (1) Duke Huan of Ch'i, (2) Duke Wên of Chin, (3) Duke Hsiang of Sung, (4) Prince Chuang of Ch'u, and (5) Duke Mu of Ch'in. Their reigns covered the period 685–591 B.C.

54. When a warlike prince attacks a powerful state, his generalship shows itself in preventing the concentration of the enemy's forces. He overawes his opponents, and their allies are prevented from joining against him.

Mei Yao-ch'ên constructs one of the chains of reasoning that are so much affected by the Chinese: "In attacking a powerful state, if you can divide her forces, you will have a superiority in strength; if you have a superiority in strength, you will overawe the enemy; if you overawe the enemy, the neighbouring states will be frightened; and if the neighbouring states are frightened, the enemy's allies will be prevented from joining her." . . .

Ch'ên Hao and Chang Yü take the sentence in quite another way. The former says: "Powerful though a prince may be, if he attacks a large state, he will be unable to raise enough troops, and must rely to some extent on external aid; if he dispenses with this, and with overweening confidence in his own strength, simply tries to intimidate the enemy, he will surely be defeated." Chang Yü puts his view thus: "If we recklessly attack a large state, our own people will be discontented and hang back. But if (as will then be the case) our display of military force is inferior by half to that of the enemy, the other chieftains will take fright and refuse to join us."

In seizing a state, the usurper ought to examine closely into all those injuries which it is necessary for him to inflict, and to do them all at one stroke, so as not to have to repeat them daily. Thus, by not unsettling men, he will be able to reassure them, and win them to himself by benefits. He who does otherwise, either from timidity or evil advice, is always compelled to keep the knife in his hand.

Niccolò Machiavelli, *The Prince* (1532)

---

55. Hence he does not strive to ally himself with all and sundry, nor does he foster the power of other states. He carries out his own secret designs, keeping his antagonists in awe.

The train of thought [according to Li Ch'üan] appears to be this: Secure against a combination of his enemies, "he can afford to reject entangling alliances and simply pursue his own secret designs, his prestige enabling him to dispense with external friendships."

Thus he is able to capture their cities and overthrow their kingdoms.

This paragraph, though written many years before the Ch'in State became a serious menace, is not a bad summary of the policy by which the famous Six Chancellors gradually paved the way for her final triumph under Shih Huang Ti. Chang Yü, following up his previous note, thinks that Sun Tzu is condemning this attitude of cold-blooded selfishness and haughty isolation. He again refers to the warlike prince once more, thus making it appear that in the end he is bound to succumb.

---

56. Bestow rewards without regard to rule,

Wu Tzu less wisely says: "Let advance be richly rewarded and retreat be heavily punished."

---

issue orders without regard to previous arrangements;

"In order to prevent treachery," says Wang Hsi. The general meaning is made clear by Ts'ao Kung's quotations from the *Ssu-ma Fa* [a military treatise thought to be from the 6th century B.C.]: "Give instructions only on sighting the enemy; give rewards only when you see deserving deeds." . . . Ts'ao Kung's paraphrase I take to mean: "The final instructions you give to your army should not correspond with those that have been previously posted up." Chang Yü simplifies this into "your arrangements should not be divulged beforehand." And Chia Lin says: "There should be no fixity in your rules and arrangements." Not only is there danger in letting your plans be known, but war often necessitates the entire reversal of them at the last moment.

---

and you will be able to handle a whole army as though you had to do with but a single man.

57. Confront your soldiers with the deed itself; never let them know your design.

Literally, "do not tell them words"; *i.e.*, do not give your reasons for any order. Lord Mansfield once told a junior colleague to "give no reasons" for his decisions, and the maxim is even more applicable to a general than to a judge. Capt. Calthrop translates this sentence with beautiful simplicity: "Orders should direct the soldiers." That is all.

William Murray, first Earl of Mansfield (1705–1793) was a British chief justice known for his unpopular prosecutions of rebel Irish lords and certain libel cases, which led to the burning of his home during the Gordon Riots.   DG

When the outlook is bright, bring it before their eyes; but tell them nothing when the situation is gloomy.

58. Place your army in deadly peril, and it will survive; plunge it into desperate straits, and it will come off in safety.

These words of Sun Tzu were once quoted by Han Hsin in explanation of the tactics he employed in one of his most brilliant battles. . . . In 204 B.C., he was sent against the army of Chao, and halted ten miles from the mouth of the Ching-hsing pass, where the enemy had mustered in full force. Here, at midnight, he detached a body of 2000 light cavalry, every man of which was furnished with a red flag. Their instructions were to make their way through narrow defiles and keep a secret watch on the enemy. "When the men of Chao see me in full flight," Han Hsin said, "they will abandon their fortifications and give chase. This must be the sign for you to rush in, pluck down the Chao standards and set up the red banners of Han in their stead."

Turning then to his other officers, he remarked: "Our adversary holds a strong position, and is not likely to come out and attack us until he sees the standard and drums of the commander-in-chief, for fear I should turn back and escape through the mountains." So saying, he first of all sent out a division consisting of 10,000 men, and ordered them to form in line of battle with their backs to the River Ti. Seeing this manœuvre, the whole army of Chao broke into loud laughter.

By this time it was broad daylight, and Han Hsin, displaying the generalissimo's flag, marched out of the pass with drums beating, and was immediately engaged by the enemy. A great battle followed, lasting for some time; until at length Han Hsin and his colleague Chang Ni, leaving drums and banner on the field, fled to the division on the river bank, where another fierce battle was raging. The enemy rushed out to pursue them and to secure the trophies, thus denuding their ramparts of men; but the two generals succeeded in joining the other army, which was fighting with the utmost desperation. The time had now come for the 2000 horsemen to play their part.

As soon as they saw the men of Chao following up their advantage, they galloped behind the deserted walls, tore up the enemy's flags and replaced them by those of Han. When the Chao army turned back from the pursuit, the sight of these red flags struck them with terror. Convinced that the Hans had got in and overpowered their king, they broke up in wild disorder, every effort of their leader to stay the panic being in vain. Then the Han army fell on them from both sides and completed the rout, killing a great number and capturing the rest, amongst whom was King Ya himself. . . .

After the battle, some of Han Hsin's officers came to him and said: "In *The Art of War*, we are told to have a hill or tumulus on the right rear, and a river or marsh on the left front. [This appears to be a blend of Sun Tzu and T'ai Kung. See chapter IX, paragraph 9, and note.] You, on the contrary, ordered us to draw up our troops with the river at our back. Under these conditions, how did you manage to gain the victory?"

The general replied, "I fear you gentlemen have not studied *The Art of War* with sufficient care. Is it not written there: '*Plunge your army into desperate straits and it will come off in safety; place it in deadly peril and it will survive*'? Had I taken the usual course, I should never have been able to bring my colleagues round. What says the Military Classic?—'Swoop down on the market-place and drive the men off to fight' [This passage does not appear in the present text of *The Art of War*]. If I had not placed my troops in a position where they were obliged to fight for their lives, but had allowed each man to follow his own discretion, there would have been a general *débandade*, and it would have been impossible to do anything with them." The officers admitted the force of his argument, and said, "These are higher tactics than we should have been capable of."

59. For it is precisely when a force has fallen into harm's way that it is capable of striking a blow for victory.

Danger has a bracing effect.

60. Success in warfare is gained by carefully accommodating ourselves to the enemy's purpose.

Ts'ao Kung says: "Feign stupidity"—by an appearance of yielding and falling in with the enemy's wishes. Chang Yü's note makes the meaning clear: "If the enemy shows an inclination to advance, lure him on to do so; if he is anxious to retreat, delay on purpose that he may carry out his intention." The object is to make him remiss and contemptuous before we deliver our attack.

---

61. By persistently hanging on the enemy's flank, we shall succeed in the long run in killing the commander-in-chief.

[The last is] always a great point with the Chinese.

---

62. This is called ability to accomplish a thing by sheer cunning.
63. On the day that you take up your command, block the frontier passes, destroy the official tallies,

[The official tallies were] used at city-gates and on the frontier. They were tablets of bamboo or wood, one half of which was issued as a permit or passport by the official in charge of a gate. When this half was returned to him, within a fixed period, he was authorised to open the gate and let the traveller through.

Not unlike our passports and visas for visiting other countries today.

DG

---

and stop the passage of all emissaries.

Either to or from the enemy's country.

---

64. Be stern in the council-chamber,

Show no weakness, and insist on your plans being ratified by the sovereign.

---

so that you may control the situation.

Mei Yao-ch'ên . . . understands the whole sentence to mean: Take the strictest precautions to ensure secrecy in your deliberations.

---

65. If the enemy leaves a door open, you must rush in.

66. Forestall your opponent by seizing what he holds dear, and subtly contrive to time his arrival on the ground.

Ch'ên Hao's explanation ... is clear enough: "If I manage to seize a favourable position, but the enemy does not appear on the scene, the advantage thus obtained cannot be turned to any practical account. He who intends, therefore, to occupy a position of importance to the enemy, must begin by making an artful appointment, so to speak, with his antagonist, and cajole him into going there as well."

Mei Yao-ch'ên explains that this "artful appointment" is to be made through the medium of the enemy's own spies, who will carry back just the amount of information that we choose to give them. Then, having cunningly disclosed our intentions, "we must manage, though starting after the enemy, to arrive before him" (chapter VII, paragraph 4). We must start after him in order to ensure his marching thither; we must arrive before him in order to capture the place without trouble.

———

67. Walk in the path defined by rule,

[The Chinese character] stands for "a marking-line," hence a rule of conduct [following the rules of the philosopher Mencius]. Ts'ao Kung explains it by the similar metaphor "square and compasses." The baldness of the sentiment rather inclines me to favour the reading adopted by Chia Lin, ... which yields an exactly opposite sense, namely: "Discard hard and fast rules."

Chia Lin says: "Victory is the only thing that matters, and this cannot be achieved by adhering to conventional canons." It is unfortunate that this variant rests on very slight authority, for the sense yielded is certainly much more satisfactory. Napoleon, as we know, according to the veterans of the old school whom he defeated, won his battles by violating every accepted canon of warfare.

———

and accommodate yourself to the enemy until you can fight a decisive battle.

Tu Mu says: "Conform to the enemy's tactics until a favourable opportunity offers; then come forth and engage in a battle that shall prove decisive."

———

68. At first, then, exhibit the coyness of a maiden, until the enemy gives you an opening; afterwards emulate the rapidity of a running hare, and it will be too late for the enemy to oppose you.

As the hare is noted for its extreme timidity, the comparison hardly appears felicitous. But of course Sun Tzu was thinking only of its speed. The words have been taken to mean: You must flee from the enemy as quickly as an escaping hare; but this is rightly rejected by Tu Mu.

XII.
THE ATTACK BY FIRE

I love the smell of napalm in the morning.
Lt. Col. Bill Kilgore in *Apocalypse Now*, screenplay by John Milius
(1976)

♦ ♦ ♦

Rather more than half the chapter (paragraphs 1–13) is devoted to the subject of fire, after which the author branches off into other topics.

1. Sun Tzu said: There are five ways of attacking with fire. The first is to burn soldiers in their camp;

Li Ch'üan says: "Set fire to the camp, and kill the soldiers" (when they try to escape from the flames). Pan Ch'ao, sent on a diplomatic mission to the King of Shan-shan [see chapter XI, paragraph 51, note], found himself placed in extreme peril by the unexpected arrival of an envoy from the Hsiung-nu [the mortal enemies of the Chinese]. In consultation with his officers, he exclaimed: "Never venture, never win! [Otherwise translated: Unless you enter the tiger's lair, you cannot get hold of the tiger's cubs.] The only course open to us now is to make an assault by fire on the barbarians under cover of night, when they will not be able to discern our numbers. Profiting by their panic, we shall exterminate them completely; this will cool the King's courage and cover us with glory, besides ensuring the success of our mission."

"The officers all replied that it would be necessary to discuss the matter first with the Intendant. Pan Ch'ao then fell into a passion: 'It is to-day,' he cried, 'that our fortunes must be decided! The Intendant is only a humdrum civilian, who on hearing of our project will certainly be afraid, and everything will be brought to light. An inglorious death is no worthy fate for valiant warriors!' All then agreed to do as he wished.

"Accordingly, as soon as night came on, he and his little band quickly made their way to the barbarian camp. A strong gale was blowing at the time. Pan Ch'ao ordered ten of the party to take drums and hide behind the enemy's barracks, it being arranged that when they saw flames shoot up, they should begin drumming and yelling with all their might. The rest of his men, armed with bows and crossbows, he posted in ambuscade at the gate of the camp. He then set fire to the place from the windward side, whereupon a deafening noise of drums and shouting arose on the front and rear of the Hsiung-nu, who rushed out pell-mell in frantic disorder. Pan Ch'ao slew three of them with his own hand, while his companions cut off the heads of the envoy and thirty of his suite. The remainder, more than a hundred in all, perished in the flames.

"On the following day, Pan Ch'ao went back and informed Kuo Hsün [the Intendant] of what he had done. The latter was greatly alarmed and turned pale. But Pan Ch'ao, divining his thoughts, said with uplifted hand: 'Although you did not go with us last night, I should not think, Sir, of taking sole credit for our exploit.' This satisfied Kuo Hsün, and Pan Ch'ao, having sent for Kuang, King of Shan-shan, showed him the head of the barbarian envoy. The whole kingdom was seized with fear and trembling, which Pan Ch'ao took steps to allay by issuing a public proclamation. Then, taking the king's son as hostage, he returned to make his report to Tou Ku."

---

the second is to burn stores;

Tu Mu says: "Provisions, fuel and fodder." In order to subdue the re-bellious population of Kiangnan, Kao Kêng recommended Wên Ti of the Sui dynasty to make periodical raids and burn their stores of grain, a policy which in the long run proved entirely successful.

---

the third is to burn baggage-trains;

An example given is the destruction of Yüan Shao's waggons and im-pediments by Ts'ao Ts'ao in 200 A.D.

---

the fourth is to burn arsenals and magazines; the fifth is to hurl dropping fire amongst the enemy.

No fewer than four totally diverse explanations of this sentence are given by the commentators, not one of which is quite satisfactory. . . . The interpretation which I have adopted is that given by Tu Yu . . . : "To drop fire into the enemy's camp. The method by which this may be done is to set the tips of arrows alight by dipping them into a brazier, and then shoot them from powerful crossbows into the enemy's lines."

2. In order to carry out an attack with fire, we must have means available.

Ts'ao Kung thinks that ["means" indicates] "traitors in the enemy's camp." . . . But Ch'ên Hao is more likely to be right in saying: "We must have favourable circumstances in general, not merely traitors to help us." Chia Lin says: "We must avail ourselves of wind and dry weather."

The material for raising fire should always be kept in readiness.

[The Chinese character] is explained by Ts'ao Kung as "appliances for making fire." Tu Mu suggests "dry vegetable matter, reeds, brushwood, straw, grease, oil, etc." . . . Chang Yü says: "vessels for hoarding fire, stuff for lighting fires."

3. There is a proper season for making attacks with fire, and special days for starting a conflagration.

A fire must not be begun "recklessly" or "at haphazard."

4. The proper season is when the weather is very dry; the special days are those when the moon is in the constellation of the Sieve, the Wall, the Wing or the Cross-bar; for these four are all days of rising wind.

These are, respectively, the 7th, 14th, 27th, and 28th of the Twenty-eight Stellar Mansions, corresponding roughly to Sagittarius, Pegasus, Crater and Corvus.

5. In attacking with fire, one should be prepared to meet five possible developments:
6. (1) When fire breaks out inside the enemy's camp, respond at once with an attack from without.

7. (2) If there is an outbreak of fire, but the enemy's soldiers remain quiet, bide your time and do not attack.

The prime object of attacking with fire is to throw the enemy into confusion. If this effect is not produced, it means that the enemy is ready to receive us. Hence the necessity for caution.

———————

8. (3) When the force of the flames has reached its height, follow it up with an attack, if that is practicable; if not, stay where you are.

Ts'ao Kung says: "If you see a possible way, advance; but if you find the difficulties too great, retire."

———————

9. (4) If it is possible to make an assault with fire from without, do not wait for it to break out within, but deliver your attack at a favourable moment.

Tu Mu says that the previous paragraphs had reference to the fire breaking out (either accidentally, we may suppose, or by the agency of incendiaries) inside the enemy's camp. "But," he continues, "if the enemy is settled in a waste place littered with quantities of grass, or if he has pitched his camp in a position which can be burnt out, we must carry our fire against him at any seasonable opportunity, and not wait on in hopes of an outbreak occurring within, for fear our opponents should themselves burn up the surrounding vegetation, and thus render our own attempts fruitless."

The famous Li Ling once baffled the leader of the Hsiung-nu in this way. The latter, taking advantage of a favourable wind, tried to set fire to the Chinese general's camp, but found that every scrap of combustible vegetation in the neighbourhood had already been burnt down.

On the other hand, Po-ts'ai, a general of the Yellow Turban rebels, was badly defeated in 184 A.D. through his neglect of this simple precaution. At the head of a large army he was besieging Ch'ang-shê, which was held by Huang-fu Sung. The garrison was very small, and a general feeling of nervousness pervaded the ranks; so Huang-fu Sung called his officers together and said: "In war, there are various indirect methods of attack, and numbers do not account for everything. [The commentator here quotes from Sun Tzu, chapter V, paragraphs 5, 6 and 10.] Now the rebels have pitched their camp in the midst of thick grass which will easily burn when the wind blows. If we set fire to it at night, they will be thrown into a panic, and we can make a sortie and attack them on all sides at once, thus emulating the achievement of T'ien Tan [who used converted spies to devastating effect]."

That same evening, a strong breeze sprang up; so Huang-fu Sung instructed his soldiers to bind reeds together into torches and mount guard on the city walls, after which he sent out a band of daring men, who stealthily made their way through the lines and started the fire with loud shouts and yells. Simultaneously, a glare of light shot up from the city-walls, and Huang-fu Sung, sounding his drums, led a rapid charge, which threw the rebels into confusion and put them into headlong flight.

----

10. (5) When you start a fire, be to windward of it. Do not attack from the leeward.

Chang Yü, following Tu Yu, says: "When you make a fire, the enemy will retreat away from it; if you oppose his retreat and attack him then, he will fight desperately, which will not conduce to your success." A rather more obvious explanation is given by Tu Mu: "If the wind is in the east, begin burning to the east of the enemy, and follow up the attack yourself from that side. If you start the fire on the east side, and then attack from the west, you will suffer in the same way as your enemy."

----

11. A wind that rises in the daytime lasts long, but a night breeze soon falls.

[Compare this] to Lao Tzu's saying: "A violent wind does not last the space of a morning" (*Tao Té Ching*, chapter 23). Mei Yao-ch'ên and Wang Hsi say: "A day breeze dies down at nightfall, and a night breeze at daybreak. This is what happens as a general rule." The phenomenon observed may be correct enough, but how this sense is to be obtained is not apparent.

----

12. In every army, the five developments connected with fire must be known, the movements of the stars calculated, and a watch kept for the proper days.

Tu Mu's commentary . . . : "We must make calculations as to the paths of the stars, and watch for the days on which wind will rise, before making our attack with fire." Chang Yü [says]: "We must not only know how to assail our opponents with fire, but also be on our guard against similar attacks from them."

———————

13. Hence those who use fire as an aid to the attack show intelligence; those who use water as an aid to the attack gain an accession of strength.

14. By means of water, an enemy may be intercepted, but not robbed of all his belongings.

Ts'ao Kung's note is: "We can merely obstruct the enemy's road or divide his army, but not sweep away all his accumulated stores." Water can do useful service, but it lacks the terrible destructive power of fire. This is the reason, Chang Yü concludes, why the former is dismissed in a couple of sentences, whereas the attack by fire is discussed in detail. Wu Tzu speaks thus of the two elements: "If an army is encamped on low-lying marshy ground, from which the water cannot run off, and where the rainfall is heavy, it may be submerged by a flood. If an army is encamped in wild marsh lands thickly overgrown with weeds and brambles, and visited by frequent gales, it may be exterminated by fire."

———————

15. Unhappy is the fate of one who tries to win his battles and succeed in his attacks without cultivating the spirit of enterprise; for the result is waste of time and general stagnation.

This is one of the most perplexing passages in [*The Art of War*]. . . . Ts'ao Kung says: "Rewards for good service should not be deferred a single day." And Tu Mu: "If you do not take opportunity to advance and reward the deserving, your subordinates will not carry out your commands, and disaster will ensue." . . .

For several reasons, however, and in spite of the formidable array of scholars on the other side, I prefer the interpretation suggested by Mei Yao-ch'ên, whose words I will quote: "Those who want to make sure of succeeding in their battles and assaults must seize the favourable moments when they come and not shrink on occasion from heroic measures: that is to say, they must resort to such means of attack as fire, water and the like. What they must not do, and what will prove fatal, is to sit still and simply hold on to the advantages they have got."

———————

16. Hence the saying: The enlightened ruler lays his plans well ahead; the good general cultivates his resources.

The meaning seems to be that the ruler lays plans which the general must show resourcefulness in carrying out. . . . Tu Mu [offers this quotation from another commentator]: "The warlike prince controls his soldiers by his authority, knits them together by good faith, and by rewards makes them serviceable. If faith decays, there will be disruption; if rewards are deficient, commands will not be respected."

17. Move not unless you see an advantage; use not your troops unless there is something to be gained; fight not unless the position is critical.

Sun Tzu may at times appear to be over-cautious, but he never goes so far in that direction as the remarkable passage in the *Tao Té Ching*, chapter 69: "I dare not take the initiative, but prefer to act on the defensive; I dare not advance an inch, but prefer to retreat a foot."

18. No ruler should put troops into the field merely to gratify his own spleen; no general should fight a battle simply out of pique.

19. If it is to your advantage, make a forward move; if not, stay where you are.

This is repeated from chapter XI, paragraph 17. Here I feel convinced that it is an interpolation.

20. Anger may in time change to gladness; vexation may be succeeded by content.

21. But a kingdom that has once been destroyed can never come again into being;

The Wu State was destined to be a melancholy example of this saying.

nor can the dead ever be brought back to life.

22. Hence the enlightened ruler is heedful, and the good general full of caution. This is the way to keep a country at peace and an army intact.

用 間 篇

XIII.
THE USE OF SPIES

———⟨∽⟩———

When you conceal your will from others, that is Thick. When you impose your will on others, that is Black.
    Lee Zhong Wu, *Thick Face, Black Heart* (1911)

✦ ✦ ✦

The evolution of the meaning "spy" is worth considering for a moment, provided it be understood that this is very doubtful ground. . . . [It is defined elsewhere] as "a crack" or "chink," and on the whole we may accept Hsü Ch'ieh's analysis as not unduly fanciful: "At night, a *door* is shut; if, when it is shut, the light of the *moon* is visible, it must come through a *chink*." From this it is an easy step to the meaning "space between," or simply "between," as for example in the phrase "to act as a secret spy between enemies." . . . Another possible theory is that the word may first have come to mean "to peep," which would naturally be suggested by "crack" or "crevice," and afterwards the man who peeps, or spy.

———————

1. Sun Tzu said: Raising a host of a hundred thousand men and marching them great distances entails heavy loss on the people and a drain on the resources of the State. The daily expenditure will amount to a thousand ounces of silver. There will be commotion at home and abroad, and men will drop down exhausted on the highways.

Chang Yü has the note: "We may be reminded of the saying: 'On serious ground, gather in plunder' [chapter XI, paragraph 13]. Why then should carriage and transportation cause exhaustion on the highways?—The answer is, that not victuals alone, but all sorts of munitions of war have to be conveyed to the army. Besides, the injunction to 'forage on the enemy' only means that when an army is deeply engaged in hostile territory, scarcity of food must be provided against. Hence, without being solely dependent on the enemy for corn, we must forage in order that there may be an uninterrupted flow of supplies. Then, again, there are places like salt deserts, where provisions being unobtainable, supplies from home cannot be dispensed with."

As many as seven hundred thousand families will be impeded in their labour.

Mei Yao-ch'ên says: "Men will be lacking at the plough-tail." The allusion is to the system of dividing land into nine parts, . . . each consisting of about 15 acres, the plot in the center being cultivated on behalf of the State by the tenants of the other eight. It was here also, as Tu Mu tells us, that their cottages were built and a well sunk, to be used by all in common. . . . In time of war, one of the families had to serve in the army, while the other seven contributed to its support. Thus, by a levy of 100,000 men (reckoning one able-bodied soldier to each family), the husbandry of 700,000 families would be affected.

---

2. Hostile armies may face each other for years, striving for the victory which is decided in a single day. This being so, to remain in ignorance of the enemy's condition simply because one grudges the outlay of a hundred ounces of silver in honours and emoluments

"For spies" is of course the meaning, though it would spoil the effect of this curiously elaborate exordium if spies were actually mentioned at this point.

---

is the height of inhumanity.

Sun Tzu's argument is certainly ingenious. He begins by adverting to the frightful misery and vast expenditure of blood and treasure which war always brings in its train. Now, unless you are kept informed of the enemy's condition, and are ready to strike at the right moment, a war may drag on for years. The only way to get this information is to employ spies, and it is impossible to obtain trustworthy spies unless they are properly paid for their services. But it is surely false economy to grudge a comparatively trifling amount for this purpose, when every day that the war lasts eats up an incalculably greater sum. This grievous burden falls on the shoulders of the poor, and hence Sun Tzu concludes that to neglect the use of spies is nothing less than a crime against humanity.

3. One who acts thus is no leader of men, no present help to his sovereign, no master of victory.

This idea, that the true object of war is peace, has its root in the national temperament of the Chinese. Even so far back as 597 B.C., these memorable words were uttered by Prince Chuang of the Ch'u State: "The character for 'prowess' is made up of [the ideographs for] 'to stay' and 'a spear' (cessation of hostilities). Military prowess is seen in the repression of cruelty, the calling in of weapons, the preservation of the appointment of Heaven, the firm establishment of merit, the bestowal of happiness on the people, putting harmony between the princes, the diffusion of wealth."

4. Thus, what enables the wise sovereign and the good general to strike and conquer, and achieve things beyond the reach of ordinary men, is *foreknowledge*.

That is, knowledge of the enemy's dispositions, and what he means to do.

5. Now this foreknowledge cannot be elicited from spirits;

"by prayers or sacrifices," says Chang Yü.

it cannot be obtained inductively from experience,

Tu Mu's note makes the meaning clear. . . . "[knowledge of the enemy] cannot be gained by reasoning from other analogous cases."

nor by any deductive calculation.

Li Ch'üan says: "Quantities like length, breadth, distance and magnitude, are susceptible of exact mathematical determination; human actions cannot be so calculated."

6. Knowledge of the enemy's dispositions can only be obtained from other men.

Mei Yao-ch'ên has rather an interesting note: "Knowledge of the spirit-world is to be obtained by divination; information in natural science may be sought by inductive reasoning; the laws of the universe can be verified by mathematical calculation: but the dispositions of an enemy are ascertainable through spies and spies alone."

7. Hence the use of spies, of whom there are five classes: (1) Local spies; (2) inward spies; (3) converted spies; (4) doomed spies; (5) surviving spies.
8. When these five kinds of spy are all at work, none can discover the secret system.

[The Chinese] is explained by Tu Mu as "the way in which facts leak out and dispositions are revealed."

This is called "divine manipulation of the threads."

Mei Yao-ch'ên's paraphrase shows that what is meant is the *control* of a number of threads.

It is the sovereign's most precious faculty.

[General Baden-Powell writes:] "Cromwell, one of the greatest and most practical of all cavalry leaders, had officers styled 'scout masters,' whose business it was to collect all possible information regarding the enemy, through scouts and spies, etc., and much of his success in war was traceable to the previous knowledge of the enemy's moves thus gained" [*Aids to Scouting*].

9. Having *local spies* means employing the services of the inhabitants of a district.

Tu Mu says: "In the enemy's country, win people over by kind treatment, and use them as spies."

_____

[General George] Crook realized that no American soldier would be able to compete with the Apache warriors on a man-to-man basis in the field of endurance.... Recognizing the problem, Crook recruited scouts on a scale never before employed in order that he would have fighting troops with the necessary individual endurance and "know how" to fight Indians on their own terms. Navahos, Pimas, and friendly Apaches were hired.

> Lt. Col. Donald V. Rattan, "Antiguerrilla Operations: A Case Study from History"(1960)

_____

10. Having *inward spies*, making use of officials of the enemy.

[The Chinese term] includes both civil and military officials. Tu Mu enumerates the following classes as likely to do good service in this respect: "Worthy men who have been degraded from office, criminals who have undergone punishment; also, favourite concubines who are greedy for gold, men who are aggrieved at being in subordinate positions, or who have been passed over in the distribution of posts, others who are anxious that their side should be defeated in order that they may have a chance of displaying their ability and talents, fickle turncoats who always want to have a foot in each boat.

"Officials of these several kinds," he continues, "should be secretly approached and bound to one's interests by means of rich presents. In this way you will be able to find out the state of affairs in the enemy's country, ascertain the plans that are being formed against you, and moreover disturb the harmony and create a breach between the sovereign and his ministers."

The necessity for extreme caution, however, in dealing with "inward spies," appears from an historical incident related by Ho Shih: "Lo Shang, Governor of I-chou, sent his general Wei Po to attack the rebel Li Hsiung of Shu in his stronghold at P'i. After each side had experienced a number of victories and defeats, Li Hsiung had recourse to the services of a certain P'o-t'ai, a native of Wu-tu. He began by having him whipped until the blood came, and then sent him off to Lo Shang, whom he was to delude by offering to co-operate with him from inside the city, and to give a fire signal at the right moment for making a general assault. Lo Shang, confiding in these promises, marched out all his best troops, and placed Wei Po and others at their head with orders to attack at P'o-t'ai's bidding.

"Meanwhile, Li Hsiung's general, Li Hsiang, had prepared an ambuscade on their line of march; and P'o-t'ai, having reared long scaling-ladders against the city walls, now lighted the beacon fire. Wei Po's men raced up on seeing the signal and began climbing the ladders as fast as they could, while others were drawn up by ropes lowered from above. More than a hundred of Lo Shang's soldiers entered the city in this way, every one of whom was forthwith beheaded. Li Hsiung then charged with all his forces, both inside and outside the city, and routed the enemy completely." [This happened in 303 A.D.]

---

11. Having *converted spies*, getting hold of the enemy's spies and using them for our own purposes.

By means of heavy bribes and liberal promises detaching them from the enemy's service, and inducing them to carry back false information, as well as to spy in turn on their own countrymen. . . .

Ho Shih notes three occasions on which converted spies were used with conspicuous success: (1) by T'ien Tan in his defence of Chi-mo [chapter IX, paragraph 24, note]; (2) by Chao Shê on his march to O-yü [chapter VII, paragraph 4, note]; and (3) by the wily Fan Chü in 260 B.C., when Lien P'o was conducting a defensive campaign against Ch'in: The King of Chao strongly disapproved of Lien P'o's cautious and dilatory methods, which had been unable to avert a series of minor disasters, and therefore lent a ready ear to the reports of his spies, who had secretly gone over to the enemy and were already in Fan Chü's pay. They said: "The only thing which causes Ch'in anxiety is lest Chao Kua should be made general. Lien P'o they consider an easy opponent, who is sure to be vanquished in the long run."

Now this Chao Kua was a son of the famous Chao Shê. From his boyhood, he had been wholly engrossed in the study of war and military matters, until at last he came to believe that there was no commander in the whole Empire who could stand against him. His father was much disquieted by this overweening conceit, and the flippancy with which he spoke of such a serious thing as war, and solemnly declared that if ever Kua were appointed general, he would bring ruin on the armies of Chao. This was the man who, in spite of earnest protests from his own mother and the veteran statesman Lin Hsiang-ju, was now sent to succeed Lien P'o.

Needless to say, he proved no match for the redoubtable Po Ch'i and the great military power of Ch'in. He fell into a trap by which his army was divided into two and his communications cut; and after a desperate resistance lasting 46 days, during which the famished soldiers devoured one another, he was himself killed by an arrow, and his whole force, amounting it is said, to 400,000 men, ruthlessly put to the sword.

12. Having *doomed spies*, doing certain things openly for purposes of deception, and allowing our own spies to know of them and report them to the enemy.

Tu Yu gives the best exposition of the meaning: "We ostentatiously do things calculated to deceive our own spies, who must be led to believe that they have been unwittingly disclosed. Then, when these spies are captured in the enemy's lines, they will make an entirely false report, and the enemy will take measures accordingly, only to find that we do something quite different. The spies will thereupon be put to death." . . .

As an example of doomed spies, Ho Shih mentions the prisoners released by Pan Ch'ao in his campaign against Yarkand [chapter XI, paragraph 36, note]. He also refers to T'ang Chien, who in 630 A.D. was sent by T'ai Tsung to lull the Turkish Khan Chieh-li into fancied security, until Li Ching was able to deliver a crushing blow against him. . . .

Li I-chi played a somewhat similar part in 203 B.C., when sent by the King of Han to open peaceful negotiations with Ch'i. He has certainly more claim to be described as a [doomed spy]; for the King of Ch'i, being subsequently attacked without warning by Han Hsin, and infuriated by what he considered the treachery of Li I-chi, ordered the unfortunate envoy to be boiled alive.

13. *Surviving spies*, finally, are those who bring back news from the enemy's camp.

This is the ordinary class of spies, properly so called, forming a regular part of the army. Tu Mu says: "Your surviving spy must be a man of keen intellect, though in outward appearance a fool; of shabby exterior, but with a will of iron. He must be active, robust, endowed with physical strength and courage; thoroughly accustomed to all sorts of dirty work, able to endure hunger and cold, and to put up with shame and ignominy."

Ho Shih tells the following story of Ta-hsi Wu of the Sui dynasty: "When he was governor of Eastern Ch'in, Shên-wu of Ch'i made a hostile movement upon Sha-yüan. The Emperor T'ai Tsu sent Ta-hsi Wu to spy upon the enemy. He was accompanied by two other men. All three were on horseback and wore the enemy's uniform. When it was dark, they dismounted a few hundred feet away from the enemy's camp and stealthily crept up to listen, until they succeeded in catching the passwords used by the army. Then they got on their horses again and boldly passed through the camp under the guise of night-watchmen; and more than once, happening to come across a soldier who was committing some breach of discipline, they actually stopped to give the culprit a sound cudgelling!

"Thus they managed to return with the fullest possible information about the enemy's dispositions, and received warm commendation from the Emperor, who in consequence of their report was able to inflict a severe defeat on his adversary."

14. Hence it is that with none in the whole army are more intimate relations to be maintained than with spies.

Tu Mu and Mei Yao-ch'ên point out that the spy is privileged to enter even the general's private sleeping-tent.

None should be more liberally rewarded. In no other business should greater secrecy be preserved.

Tu Mu [says that] all communications with spies should be carried on "mouth-to-ear." . . . The following remarks on spies may be quoted from [Marshal] Turenne, who made perhaps larger use of them than any previous commander: "Spies are attached to those who give them most; he who pays them ill is never served. They should never be known to anybody; nor should they know one another. When they propose anything very material, secure their persons, or have in your possession their wives and children as hostages for their fidelity. Never communicate anything to them but what is absolutely necessary that they should know."

15. Spies cannot be usefully employed without a certain intuitive sagacity.

Mei Yao-ch'ên says: "In order to use them, one must know fact from falsehood, and be able to discriminate between honesty and double-dealing." . . . Tu Mu strangely refers these attributes to the spies themselves: "Before using spies we must assure ourselves as to their integrity of character and the extent of their experience and skill." But he continues: "A brazen face and a crafty disposition are more dangerous than mountains or rivers; it takes a man of genius to penetrate such." So that we are left in some doubt as to his real opinion on the passage.

And if, to be sure, sometimes you need to conceal a fact with words, do it in such a way that it does not become known, or, if it does become known, that you have a ready and quick defence.

> Niccolò Machiavelli, "Advice to Raffaello Girolami When He Went as Ambassador to the Emperor" (1522)

16. They cannot be properly managed without benevolence and straightforwardness.

Chang Yü [interprets the Chinese as] "not grudging them honours and pay"; "showing no distrust of their honesty." [So that the passage would read:] "When you have attracted them by substantial offers, you must treat them with absolute sincerity; then they will work for you with all their might."

17. Without subtle ingenuity of mind, one cannot make certain of the truth of their reports.

Mei Yao-ch'ên says: "Be on your guard against the possibility of spies going over to the service of the enemy."

18. Be subtle! Be subtle! and use your spies for every kind of business.
19. If a secret piece of news is divulged by a spy before the time is ripe, he must be put to death together with the man to whom the secret was told.

The Chinese here is so concise and elliptical that some expansion is necessary for the proper understanding of it. . . . Word for word [it reads]: "If spy matters are heard before [our plans] are carried out," etc. . . . The main point of Sun Tzu's injunction [must surely be that] whereas you kill the spy himself "as a punishment for letting out the secret," the object of killing the other man is only, as Ch'ên Hao puts it, "to stop his mouth" and prevent the news leaking any further. If it had already been repeated to others, this object would not be gained.

Either way, Sun Tzu lays himself open to the charge of inhumanity, though Tu Mu tries to defend him by saying that the man deserves to be put to death, for the spy would certainly not have told the secret unless the other had been at pains to worm it out of him.

Men should either be treated generously or destroyed, because they take revenge for slight injuries—for heavy ones, they cannot.
Niccolò Machiavelli, *The Prince* (1532)

---

20. Whether the object be to crush an army, to storm a city, or to assassinate an individual, it is always necessary to begin by finding out the names of the attendants,

those who wait on others, servants and retainers generally.

---

the aides-de-camp,

[Tu Yu describes them as] "those whose duty it is to keep the general supplied with information," which naturally necessitates frequent interviews with him.

---

the door-keepers and sentries of the general in command. Our spies must be commissioned to ascertain these.

As the first step, no doubt, towards finding out if any of these important functionaries can be won over by bribery.

---

21. The enemy's spies who have come to spy on us must be sought out, tempted with bribes, led away and comfortably housed. Thus they will become converted spies and available for our service.

22. It is through the information brought by the converted

spy that we are able to acquire and employ local and inward spies.

Tu Yu expands this into "through conversion of the enemy's spies we learn the enemy's condition." And Chang Yü says: "We must tempt the converted spy into our service, because it is he that knows which of the local inhabitants are greedy of gain, and which of the officials are open to corruption."

---

23. It is owing to his information, again, that we can cause the doomed spy to carry false tidings to the enemy.

[Chang Yü puts it thus:] "Because the converted spy knows how the enemy can best be deceived."

---

24. Lastly, it is by his information that the surviving spy can be used on appointed occasions.
25. The end and aim of spying in all its five varieties is knowledge of the enemy; and this knowledge can only be derived, in the first instance, from the converted spy.

He not only brings information himself, but makes it possible to use the other kinds of spy to advantage.

Hence it is essential that the converted spy be treated with the utmost liberality.
26. Of old, the rise of the Yin dynasty

Sun Tzu means the Shang dynasty, founded in 1766 B.C. Its name was changed to Yin by P'an Kêng in 1401.

---

was due to I Chih,

Better known as I Yin, the famous general and statesman who took part in Ch'êng T'ang's campaign against Chieh Kuei.

---

who had served under the Hsia. Likewise, the rise of the Chou dynasty was due to Lü Ya,

[Lü Ya was also known as] Lü Shang. [He] rose to high office under the tyrant Chou Hsin, whom he afterwards helped to overthrow. . . . He is said to have composed a treatise on war.

---

who had served under the Yin.

There is less precision in the Chinese than I have thought it well to introduce into my translation, and the commentaries on this passage are by no means explicit. But, having regard to the context, we can hardly doubt that Sun Tzu is holding up I Chih and Lü Ya as illustrious examples of the converted spy, or something closely analogous. His suggestion is, that the Hsia and Yin dynasties were upset owing to the intimate knowledge of their weaknesses and shortcomings which these former ministers were able to impart to the other side. Mei Yao-ch'ên appears to resent any such aspersion on these historic names: "I Yin and Lü Ya," he says, "were not rebels against the Government. Hsia could not employ the former, hence Yin employed him. Yin could not employ the latter, hence Chou employed him. Their great achievements were all for the good of the people."

Ho Shih is also indignant: "How should two divinely inspired men such as I and Lü have acted as common spies? Sun Tzu's mention of them simply means that the proper use of the five classes of spies is a matter which requires men of the highest mental calibre, like I and Lü, whose wisdom and capacity qualified them for the task. [His] words only emphasize this point." Ho Shih believes then that the two heroes are mentioned on account of their supposed skill in the use of spies. But this is [a] very weak [interpretation].

---

27. Hence it is only the enlightened ruler and the wise general who will use the highest intelligence of the army for purposes of spying,

Ch'ên Hao . . . points out that "the god-like wisdom of Ch'êng T'ang and Wu Wang led them to employ I Yin and Lü Shang."

---

and thereby they achieve great results.

Tu Mu closes with a note of warning: "Just as water, which carries a boat from bank to bank, may also be the means of sinking it, so reliance

ssion, they are scarcely intelligible and stand no less in
f a commentary than the text itself. . . . Ts'ao Kung is
uted author of a book on war in 100,000 odd words,
t. . . .

G Shih, c. a.d. 502–557? or possibly as early as
third century

mentary which has come down to us under this name
aratively meagre, and nothing about the author is
Even his personal name has not been recorded. . . .
amed [as the] last of the "Five Commentators," the
eing Wei Wu Ti [Ts'ao Ts'ao], Tu Mu, Ch'ên Hao
Lin.

'üan, eighth century a.d.

a well-known writer on military tactics. [One of his
has been in constant use down to the present day.
is works recounts the] lives of famous generals from
to the T'ang Dynasties. . . . He is also generally sup-
be the real author of [a] popular Taoist tract. . . . His
mostly short and to the point, and he frequently il-
is remarks by anecdotes from Chinese history. [How-
ommentaries are based on a version of the Sun Tzu
iffers considerably from those now extant.]

died 812 a.d.

ot publish a separate commentary on Sun Tzu, his
taken from the T'ung Tien, the encyclopædic trea-
Constitution which was his life-work. They are
etitions of Ts'ao Kung and Mêng Shih, besides
believed that he drew on the ancient commentaries
ing and others. . . . [The poet and commentator Tu
grandson.]

803–852 a.d.

aps best known as a poet—a bright star even in the
axy of the T'ang period. We learn from Ch'ao
at although he had no practical experience of war,
mely fond of discussing the subject, and was more-
ad in the military history of the Ch'un Ch'iu and

on spies, while productive of great results, is oft-times the cause of utter destruction."

———

Spies are a most important element in war, because on them depends an army's ability to move.

Chia Lin says that an army without spies is like a man without ears or eyes.

———

Appeni

The Commi

by Lionel
edited by Dai

Sun Tzu can boast an except
roll of commentators, which
sic. . . .

1. Ts'ao Ts'ao, also known
WEI WU TI, A.D. 155–220

There is hardly any room for
tary on Sun Tzu actually can
dinary man, whose biography
romance. One of the greates
has seen, and Napoleonic in
especially famed for the ma
which has found expression
and Ts'ao Ts'ao will appea
he was a great captain who

measured his strength aga
Yüan, father and son, and
divided the Empire of Ha
self king. It is recorded
held by Wei on the eve o
his calculations ready; th
did not lose one battle i
in any particular saw the
to flight.

Ts'ao Kung's notes on S
so thoroughly character
history, that it is hard i
of a mere *littérateur*.

2. MÊN
the
The co
is comp
known.
[H]e is
others b
and Chi

3. Li C
[He] was
treatises]
[One of
the Chou
posed to
notes are
lustrates
ever, his
text that

4. Tu Yu
[He] did
notes bein
tise on the
largely rep
which it is
of Wang L
Mu was his

5. Tu Mu,
[He] is perh
glorious ga
Kung-wu th
he was extre
over well re

Chan Kuo eras. His notes, therefore, are well worth attention. They are very copious, and replete with historical parallels. The gist of Sun Tzu's work is thus summarised by him: "Practise benevolence and justice, but on the other hand make full use of artifice and measures of expediency." He further declared that all the military triumphs and disasters of the thousand years which had elapsed since Sun Wu's death would, upon examination, be found to uphold and corroborate, in every particular, the maxims contained in his book. . . .

6. Ch'ën Hao, T'ang Dynasty (618–907 a.d.)
[He] appears to have been a contemporary of Tu Mu. Ch'ao Kung-wu says that he was impelled to write a new commentary on Sun Tzu because Ts'ao Kung's on the one hand was too obscure and subtle, and that of Tu Mu on the other too long-winded and diffuse. Ou-yang Hsiu, writing in the middle of the 11th century, calls Ts'ao Kung, Tu Mu and Ch'ên Hao the three chief commentators on Sun Tzu. . . . [Ch'ên's] commentary, though not lacking in merit, must rank below those of his predecessors.

7. Chia Lin, no dates, but he lived during the T'ang dynasty (618–907 a.d.)
[His commentary on Sun Tzu] is of somewhat scanty texture, and in point of quality, too, perhaps the least valuable of the eleven.

8. Mei Yao-ch'ën, 1002–1060
[C]ommonly known by his "style" as Mei Shêng-yü, [he] was, like Tu Mu, a poet of distinction. His commentary was published with a laudatory preface by the great Ou-yang Hsiu, from which we may cull the following:

> Later scholars have misread Sun Tzu, distorting his words and trying to make them square with their own one-sided views. Thus, though commentators have not been lacking, only a few have proved equal to the task. My friend Shêng-yü has not fallen into this mistake. In attempting to provide a critical commentary for Sun Tzu's work, he does not lose sight of the fact that these sayings were intended for states engaged in in-

ternecine warfare; that the author is not concerned with the military conditions prevailing under the sovereigns of the three ancient dynasties (the Hsia, the Shang, and the Chou), nor with the nine punitive measures prescribed to the Minister of War. Again, Sun Wu loved brevity of diction, but his meaning is always deep. Whether the subject be marching an army, or handling soldiers, or estimating the enemy, or controlling the forces of victory, it is always systematically treated; the sayings are bound together in strict logical sequence, though this has been obscured by commentators who have probably failed to grasp their meaning. In his own commentary, Mei Shêng-yü has brushed aside all the obstinate prejudices of these critics, and has tried to bring out the true meaning of Sun Tzu himself. In this way, the clouds of confusion have been dispersed and the sayings made clear. I am convinced that the present work deserves to be handed down side by side with the three great commentaries; and for a great deal that they find in the sayings, coming generations will have constant reason to thank my friend Shêng-yü.

Making some allowance for the exuberance of friendship, I am inclined to endorse this favourable judgment, and would certainly place him above Ch'ên Hao in order of merit.

9. WANG HSI, SUNG DYNASTY (960–1279 A.D.)
[He] is decidedly original in some of his interpretations, but much less judicious than Mei Yao-ch'ên, and on the whole not a very trustworthy guide. He is fond of comparing his own commentary with that of Ts'ao Kung, but the comparison is not always flattering to him. We learn from Ch'ao Kung-wu that Wang Hsi revised the ancient text of Sun Tzu, filling up lacunæ and correcting mistakes.

10. HO YEN-HSI, SUNG DYNASTY (960–1279 A.D.)
[There is some controversy over his personal name and biography.] . . . he appears simply as Ho Shih in the *Yü Hai*, and [it has been said] that his personal name is unknown. . . . [His] commentary . . . "contains helpful additions" here and there, but is chiefly remarkable for the copious extracts taken, in adapted form, from the dynastic histories and other sources.

11. CHANG YÜ, LATE SUNG DYNASTY?

The list closes with a commentator of no great originality perhaps, but gifted with admirable powers of lucid exposition. His
commentary is based on that of Ts'ao Kung, whose terse sentences he contrives to expand and develop in masterly fashion.
Without Chang Yü, it is safe to say that much of Ts'ao Kung's
commentary would have remained cloaked in its pristine ob-
scurity and therefore valueless. His work . . . finds a niche in
the *T'ung Chih*, [a literary history] which also names him as the
author of the "Lives of Famous Generals."

It is rather remarkable that the last-named four should all
have flourished within so short a space of time. Ch'ao Kung-
wu accounts for it by saying,

> During the early years of the Sung dynasty the Empire enjoyed
> a long spell of peace, and men ceased to practise the art of
> war. But when [Chao] Yüan-hao's rebellion came (1038–42)
> and the frontier generals were defeated time after time, the
> Court made strenuous enquiry for men skilled in war, and mil-
> itary topics became the vogue amongst all the high officials.
> Hence it is that the commentators of Sun Tzu in our dynasty
> belong mainly to that period.

FOR FURTHER READING

The first thing to know about Sun Tzu, author of *The Art of War*, is that he would be amazed and horrified to learn that you are reading his book! As Burton Watson, the great translator of classical Chinese and Japanese literature, points out, it was assumed in ancient China "that anyone to whom the text was transmitted would receive instruction in its meaning when he received the text." Writing still carried the charge of the supernatural, of sacred knowledge. Only a warrior scholar could have composed this text, and only those who were initiated could have received it. The following list of books and sources is offered for today's readers who would like to gain a deeper comprehension of *The Art of War* in the fullness of how it should be understood.

When Sun Tzu composed his treatise, wars were dictated by kings and run by elites. The world over, they were fought for territory or other gain. Education was predicated on knowledge of the "classics" that, West or East, focused in large part on a literature bound up in tales of war. Thoroughgoing training in strategy was part of a proper education, and dabbling in military history was a common hobby of members of the upper classes and informed their rhetorical oratory.

The education of the upper classes continued to emphasize the classics and war through the late nineteenth century, when our translator, Lionel Giles, began his singular work in England. While he labored to bridge the vast differences in history, language, and customs between his readers and Sun Tzu, Giles was in important respects working from a similar mindset: He was well-read in the classics of Greece and Rome, deeply trained in military history, and aware of the foibles of contemporary politics and policies—not to mention being a great sinologist in his own right and the son of another.

But today, as armchair warriors, we must search Western and Eastern sources for the references that will bring Sun Tzu's text to meaningful life. This list of suggested sources, which ranges over a number of disciplines, includes works written by the founders of Western civilized thought at the time Sun Tzu was composing *The Art of War* and works with insights into the lives of those who fight. The section concludes with a list of Internet sources that lead through hyperlinks to a suite of related disciplines, and films that offer graphic depictions of the complexities of the ancient Asian warrior ethic.

Books

Asian Studies

de Bary, William Theodore, Wing-tsit Chan, and Burton Watson, eds. *Sources of Chinese Tradition*. Vol. 1 in the series *Introduction to Oriental Civilizations*. New York: Columbia University Press, 1964. One of the great research tools for students of Asian affairs.

Hawkes, David. *Ch'u Tz'u: The Songs of the South*. Oxford: Clarendon Press, 1959. Beautiful translations of songs from one of the five Confucian classics, *The Book of Songs*.

Kitagawa, Joseph M., ed. *The Religious Traditions of Asia*. New York: Macmillan, 1989.

Payne, Robert. *Mao Tse-Tung*. 1950. New York: Weybright and Talley, 1969. A superlative biography and fount of unusual insights, historical comparisons, personal encounters, poetry, and research on the military strategies of one of the seminal figures of the twentieth century. Mao used his knowledge of *The Art of War* to fend off the invading Japanese in World War II and to beat Chiang Kai-chek, another aficionado of Sun Tzu, in China's civil war. Payne provides extraordinary sociological insight into life in China and the workings of military strategy.

———. *A Rage for China*. New York: Holt, Rinehart and Winston, 1977. Reminiscences of a witness to some of the most important events of twentieth-century Chinese history.

———. *The White Pony*. New York: John Day, 1947. Songs and poetry that would have been heard by Sun Tzu. Called *Ch'u* songs and *Yüeh fu* ballads, they are translated by Payne and some of China's best mid-twentieth-century poets and scholars.

Waley, Arthur. *The Book of Songs*. Boston, New York: Houghton Mifflin, 1937. Also known as *The Book of Odes*. One of the five Classics of Confucius, translated for the general reader, and one of the first—and perhaps the most accessible, after Payne's *The White Pony*—of all early Chinese poetry works in English. Like Lionel Giles, Waley was a great pioneer of translation from Chinese to English.

Watson, Burton. *Early Chinese Literature*. New York: Columbia University Press, 1962. A seminal work of history and criticism; an essential research tool.

————, trans. *Courtier and Commoner in Ancient China: Selections from the History of the Former Han by Pan Ku*. New York: Columbia University Press, 1977. Pan Ku's celebrated and influential work has been a model for dynastic history since its appearance in the first century A.D. Translated by a legendary author whose scholarship is breathtaking.

————, trans. *Records of the Grand Historian of China: Translated from the Shih chi of Ssu-ma Chi'en*. 2 vols. New York: Columbia University Press, 1961. The great history of early China; sets the standard for all subsequent historical writing in the East. Filled with fascinating, sometimes amusing, often horrifying, anecdotes of life, war, and mini-biographies, this book has been compared to Plutarch's *Lives*.

Other Translations of *The Art of War*

Of the scores of versions of *The Art of War* that have been published in the United States since the 1960s, a considerable number use the book as a jumping-off point for their own purposes—mainly, how to win: in business, film-making, martial arts, litigation. Here are some of the better editions.

Ames, Roger T. *Sun Tzu: The Art of Warfare*. New York: Ballantine Books, 1993. Contains both the original Chinese text and the English translation. Ames was the first to publish a version based on the Yin Chüeh Shan text—ancient bamboo strips found in Linyi, China, in 1972; provides a fair amount of cultural and philosophical background.

222 FOR FURTHER READING

Clavell, James. *The Art of War, by Sun Tzu*. New York: Delacorte Press, 1983. The Lionel Giles version as emended and rewritten by Clavell.

Cleary, Thomas. *The Art of War*. Boston: Shambhala, 1988. Cleary is a good translator, and his introductions are superlative.

———. *The Lost Art of War*. San Francisco: HarperSanFrancisco, 1996. Also known as *The Art of War II* and *Sun Tzu II*—written by Sun Pin, said to be a descendant of Sun Tzu.

Denma Translation Group. *Sun Tzu, The Art of War: A New Translation*. Boston: Shambhala, 2001. The most recent and authoritative translation; includes valuable explanatory essays and a commentary. The translators used a version of the text known as the Yin Chüeh Shan, the oldest version ever found, dating from c.140–118 B.C.; it was copied onto thin bamboo strips, preserved for centuries, and discovered in 1972.

Griffith, Samuel B. *Sun Tzu: The Art of War*. With a foreword by B. H. Liddell Hart. New York: Oxford University Press, 1963. Griffith is an expert in the analysis of military matters who also provides an analysis of Sun Tzu's influence on Mao Tse-tung and the Japanese military. Liddell Hart is also a brilliant writer on military affairs.

Sawyer, Ralph D., and Mei-chün Lee Sawyer. *Sun Tzu: The Art of War*. New York: Barnes and Noble, 1994. For readers interested in Chinese history and military weaponry.

Wing, R. L. *The Art of Strategy*. New York: Doubleday, 1988. *The Art of War* with commentary that focuses on the strategic realm; suggests that war not be waged save to preserve one's territory.

War and Strategy

Ambrose, Stephen E. *American Heritage New History of World War II*. Revised and updated by Stephen Ambrose based on the original text by C. L. Sulzberger. New York: Viking Press, 1997.

Cairnes, William E., and David G. Chandler. *The Military Maxims of Napoleon*. New York: Da Capo Press, 1995.

Chandler updates the edition of Napoleon's maxims produced in 1901 by Cairnes and provides further commentary.

Churchill, Winston. *The Second World War*. 6 vols. London: Cassell, 1948–1954. An invaluable account by Britain's wartime prime minister and an architect of the Allied victory.

Clough, A. H., ed. *Plutarch: Lives of Noble Grecians and Romans*. Translated by John Dryden. New York: Modern Library, 1992.

Cook, Haruko Taya, and Theodore F. Cook. *Japan at War: An Oral History*. New York: New Press, 1992.

Freedman, Lawrence, ed. *War*. Oxford and New York: Oxford University Press, 1994. A formidable collection of essays by renowned scholars.

Handel, Michael I. *Masters of War: Sun Tzu, Clausewitz, and Jomini*. Portland, OR: Frank Cass, 1992. Compares Sun Tzu's approach with that of two great nineteenth-century military thinkers. General Baron Antoine-Henri de Jomini was a French-Swiss commander who served under Napoleon and later the czar; his approach to strategy focused on speed, agility, and an aggressive offense. Von Clausewitz, the great Prussian theorist, was strong on defense; he believed wars are won by attrition, inducing the enemy into massive affairs in which the last man standing wins. Handel suggests neither stands the test of time as Sun Tzu has.

Hastings, Max. *The Korean War*. New York: Simon and Schuster, 1987.

Machiavelli, Niccolò. *The Art of War*. 1521. A revised edition of the Ellis Farneworth translation; with an introduction by Neal Wood. New York: Da Capo Press, 1990.

———. *The Prince*. 1532. Translated, edited, and with an introduction by Daniel Donno. New York: Bantam Classics, 1984. Many other good editions are also available.

McClintock, Michael. *Instruments of Statecraft: U.S. Guerrilla Warfare, Counterinsurgency, and Counter-terrorism, 1940–1990*. New York: Pantheon Books, 1992. Explores principles of *The Art of War* that have intrigued U.S. guerrilla-warfare strategists for a half century.

Musashi, Miyamoto. *A Book of Five Rings*. Translated by Victor Harris. Woodstock, NY: Overlook Press, 1992. Written in 1645 by a renowned swordsman and wandering samurai (ronin), Japan's great contribution to strategic theory is recommended for those who seek mobility in a tightly structured hierarchy.

Roberts, J. M. *A Short History of the World*. New York: Oxford University Press, 1993.

Ropp, Theodore. *War in the Modern World*. Durham, NC: Duke University Press, 1959.

Sawyer, Ralph, and Mei-chun Lee Sawyer. *The Seven Military Classics of Ancient China*. Boulder, CO: Westview Press, 1993.

Tuchman, Barbara. *The Guns of August*. 1962. New York: Ballantine Books, 1994. On World War I and its inception.

Von Clausewitz, Carl. *On War*. 1833. Edited and translated by Peter Paret and Michael Howard. Princeton: Princeton University Press, 1976.

Web Sites

There are scores of relevant military websites on the Internet, and many dedicated solely to *The Art of War* and Asia studies.

www.belisarius.com: This site's primary focus is business, but it takes a decidedly military stance.

www.d-n-i.net: This is home to Defense and the National Interest, a business and military information site. It devotes considerable space to the work of legendary pilot and designer Colonel John Boyd (U.S. Air Force), who developed three influential, mathematically coherent combat theories: agility, maneuver warfare strategy, and the system referred to by the acronym OODA (observe, orient, decide, act)—all based on his experiences as a fighter pilot and his intense study of *The Art of War* and other classic works on military strategy.

www.dmoz.org/Arts/Literature/World_Literature/Chinese/ Sun_Tzu: This is the locale for Sun Tzu at the Open Directory Project (ODP). It provides scores of hyperlinks to wonderful websites dedicated to military history, Asian studies, and literature—all suggested by Sun Tzu and *The Art of War*. A valuable site for other subjects as well.

www.Sonshi.com: The best site for newly minted aficionados. With book reviews, news bulletins, and a conversational tone, it is the most accessible and provides hyperlinks to some of the better sites dedicated to Sun Tzu and Eastern philosophical systems.

www.VictoryOverWar.com: Formed by the Denma Translation Group—led by scholars Kidder Smith, an author and professor at Bowdoin College, and James Gimian, publisher of *Shambhala Sun*—this beautiful, thought-provoking site brings together important literary, philosophical, and cultural components to create a sense of Sun Tzu's larger project. The site is frequently updated.

www.vikingphoenix.com/SunTzu. Dedicated to military books and source materials in every mode.

Films

Film, granted its romanticism and lack of scholarly cachet, offers entrée, at least in simulacrum, to the world Sun Tzu wants us to understand. As works of art, films can evoke the tension, the fear, and the practical factors that plague combatants, such as incomplete information or supply lines, rotten weather, and general chaos. Moreover, when we are immersed in the clear tones of Sun Tzu's prose, it is difficult to remember the psychological atmosphere—the intrigues, the pride, and the urgency—that press the decision to fight. Movies readily deliver this atmosphere and also offer valuable insights into other cultures and other times.

With the exception of the kung-fu genre, the studios of China and Taiwan have not produced significant films for international audiences that depict the sage commander in battle or in other ways interpret the history or present the cultural backdrop of *The Art of War*. But given the Chinese national love affair with history, art, and philosophy, this will doubtless change. Meanwhile, *Crouching Tiger, Hidden Dragon* (2000), an

American production directed by Ang Lee and based on the novel by Wang Du Lu, is a brilliant exploration by a Chinese director of many of the Taoist themes in Sun Tzu. At the time of the film's release, Ang Lee said, "My team and I chose the most populist genre, the martial arts film of Hong Kong, as an instrument, a way to investigate the cultural inheritance of China . . . and the passing on of that Taoist tradition from generation to generation." He succeeded. *Crouching Tiger* also illustrates the implicit concepts of honor and duty as set forth in *The Art of War*.

Jackie Chan, director and star of countless rollicking kung-fu action movies, is another devotee of Sun Tzu and *The Art of War*. Though he has not yet fixed the title, Chan is producing a film based on Sun Tzu to debut in 2004.

Japanese cinema is especially rich in historical dramas with military themes. These films explore not just the weaponry and the approach to battle, but also the human sensibility that doubtless prompted Sun Tzu to compose his treatise. This is no surprise: When Chinese culture traveled to Japan, *The Art of War* quickly became a treasured text—so much so that the aristocracy trained in kendo (the way of the sword) and Chinese classics right up to World War II. And Sun Tzu remained every general's bible. Moreover, the Japanese suffered through their own "warring states" era, a 400-year period of interminable civil wars and unimaginable brutality among provincial lords, warrior monks, and brigands, all fighting for land and power. This era ended with the founding of the form of government known as Tokugawa Shogunate in the early seventeenth century, but it has provided authors and filmmakers with endless fodder for historical dramas and penetrating psychological explorations.

Akira Kurosawa, the great genius of twentieth-century Japanese cinema, loved to explore historico-literary subjects, but his greatest works are popular tales of a common man caught in the jaws of history. They reflect Taoist principles and the codes of chivalry underlying the decision to fight and are imbued with the ancient Japanese understanding of Sun Tzu a millennium after Sun Tzu composed his treatise. In *Seven Samurai* (1954), itinerant warriors (samurai) are hired to rescue a town beset by bandit warlords. The fight scenes, the issues of class, and the final futility of violence make this a startling and moving work. The samurai, who in this instance personify the weak and small pitted against the well-equipped and strong, use battle techniques as explicated by Sun Tzu.

Kurosawa's *Kagemusha* (1980) is set during a period of terrible interstate wars and consolidation, when a king dies and is replaced by a common thief who could be his twin. Though the action takes place long after the time of *The Art of War*, the film gives the sense of hierarchies and the laying out of plans before battle much as Sun Tzu described them. In *Sanshiro Sugata* (1945), an undisciplined young man becomes a martial arts expert and falls in love, providing viewers with a look at the principles of Sun Tzu on the personal level. Finally, *Yojimbo* (1961) tells the story of a highly skilled samurai who finds himself in a town divided between rival gangsters and who succeeds in bringing peace by adhering to the principles of Sun Tzu.